THE STATES AND THE NATION SERIES, of which this volume is a part, is designed to assist the American people in a serious look at the ideals they have espoused and the experiences they have undergone in the history of the nation. The content of every volume represents the scholarship, experience, and opinions of its author. The costs of writing and editing were met mainly by grants from the National Endowment for the Humanities, a federal agency. The project was administered by the American Association for State and Local History, a nonprofit learned society, working with an Editorial Board of distinguished editors, authors, and historians, whose names are listed below.

Pennsylvania

A Bicentennial History

Thomas C. Cochran

W. W. Norton & Company, Inc.
New York

American Association for State and Local History
Nashville

Copyright © 1978
American Association for State and Local History
Nashville, Tennessee

Published and distributed by
W. W. Norton & Company, Inc.
500 Fifth Avenue
New York, New York 10036

Library of Congress Cataloguing-in-Publication Data

Cochran, Thomas Childs, 1902–
    Pennsylvania : a Bicentennial history.

    (The States and the Nation series)
    Bibliography: p.
    Includes index.
    1. Pennsylvania—History.   I. Title.   II. Series.
F149.C7   974.8   77-15017
ISBN 0–393–05635–X

Printed in the United States of America
2 3 4 5 6 7 8 9 0

Contents

Illustrations

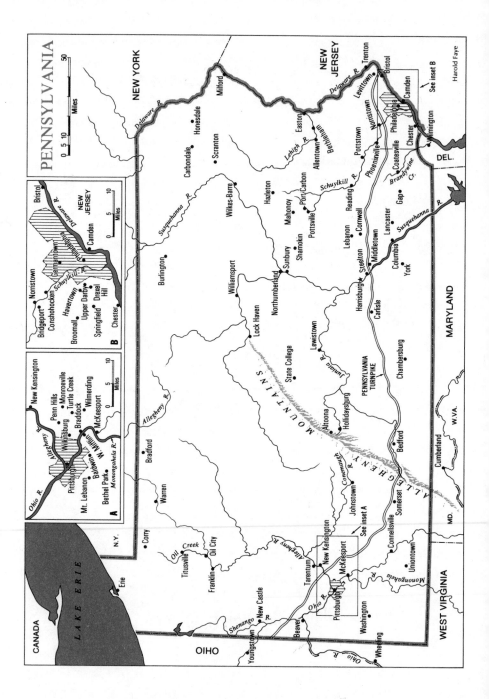

Invitation to the Reader

IN 1807, former President John Adams argued that a complete history of the American Revolution could not be written until the history of change in each state was known, because the principles of the Revolution were as various as the states that went through it. Two hundred years after the Declaration of Independence, the American nation has spread over a continent and beyond. The states have grown in number from thirteen to fifty. And democratic principles have been interpreted differently in every one of them.

We therefore invite you to consider that the history of your state may have more to do with the bicentennial review of the American Revolution than does the story of Bunker Hill or Valley Forge. The Revolution has continued as Americans extended liberty and democracy over a vast territory. John Adams was right: the states are part of that story, and the story is incomplete without an account of their diversity.

The Declaration of Independence stressed life, liberty, and the pursuit of happiness; accordingly, it shattered the notion of holding new territories in the subordinate status of colonies. The Northwest Ordinance of 1787 set forth a procedure for new states to enter the Union on an equal footing with the old. The Federal Constitution shortly confirmed this novel means of building a nation out of equal states. The step-by-step process through which territories have achieved self-government and national representation is among the most important of the Founding Fathers' legacies.

The method of state-making reconciled the ancient conflict between liberty and empire, resulting in what Thomas Jefferson called an empire for liberty. The system has worked and remains unaltered, despite enormous changes that have taken

place in the nation. The country's extent and variety now surpass anything the patriots of '76 could likely have imagined.
The United States has changed from an agrarian republic into a
highly industrial and urban democracy, from a fledgling nation
into a major world power. As Oliver Wendell Holmes remarked
in 1920, the creators of the nation could not have seen completely how it and its constitution and its states would develop.
Any meaningful review in the bicentennial era must consider
what the country has become, as well as what it was.

The new nation of equal states took as its motto *E Pluribus
Unum*—"out of many, one." But just as many peoples have
become Americans without complete loss of ethnic and cultural
identities, so have the states retained differences of character.
Some have been superficial, expressed in stereotyped images—
big, boastful Texas, "sophisticated" New York, "hillbilly"
Arkansas. Other differences have been more real, sometimes instructively, sometimes amusingly; democracy has embraced
Huey Long's Louisiana, bilingual New Mexico, unicameral Ne-
braska, and a Texas that once taxed fortunetellers and spawned
politicians called "Woodpecker Republicans" and "Skunk
Democrats." Some differences have been profound, as when
South Carolina secessionists led other states out of the Union in
opposition to abolitionists in Massachusetts and Ohio. The result was a bitter Civil War.

The Revolution's first shots may have sounded in Lexington
and Concord; but fights over what democracy should mean and
who should have independence have erupted from Pennsylvania's Gettysburg to the "Bleeding Kansas" of John Brown,
from the Alamo in Texas to the Indian battles at Montana's
Little Bighorn. Utah Mormons have known the strain of isola-
tion; Hawaiians at Pearl Harbor, the terror of attack; Georgians
during Sherman's march, the sadness of defeat and devastation.
Each state's experience differs instructively; each adds understanding to the whole.

The purpose of this series of books is to make that kind of understanding accessible, in a way that will last in value far
beyond the bicentennial fireworks. The series offers a volume
on every state, plus the District of Columbia—fifty-one, in all.

Each book contains, besides the text, a view of the state through eyes other than the author's—a "photographer's essay," in which a skilled photographer presents his own personal perceptions of the state's contemporary flavor.

We have asked authors not for comprehensive chronicles, nor for research monographs or new data for scholars. Bibliographies and footnotes are minimal. We have asked each author for a summing up—interpretive, sensitive, thoughtful, individual, even personal—of what seems significant about his or her state's history. What distinguishes it? What has mattered about it, to its own people and to the rest of the nation? What has it come to now?

To interpret the states in all their variety, we have sought a variety of backgrounds in authors themselves and have encouraged variety in the approaches they take. They have in common only these things: historical knowledge, writing skill, and strong personal feelings about a particular state. Each has wide latitude for the use of the short space. And if each succeeds, it will be by offering you, in your capacity as a *citizen* of a state *and* of a nation, stimulating insights to test against your own.

James Morton Smith
General Editor

Preface

N commissioning this series of essays in honor of the bicentennial the American Association for State and Local
History and its sponsor, the National Endowment for the
Humanities, asked the author of each state history to write on
the aspects of that state which he or she considered most no-
table. There can be little question that after the American Revolution Pennsylvania's most important contributions to the nation
were in natural resources, business institutions, and manufacturing. My half-century of interest in these developments in the
nation as a whole was one of the reasons why I was asked to
write the Pennsylvania history.

Immersion in the business and economic history of the state
has given me a new realization of its indispensable importance
in nineteenth-century industrialization. Literally without managerial, material, or technological aid from any of the surrounding states, the "business" and "industrial" revolutions would
inevitably have taken place in Pennsylvania and spread to the
rest of the nation. This means that almost up to 1900 the development of business and industry in the appropriately named
Keystone State can be a relatively local history. Only in the latter half of the nineteenth century was there an important spread
of coal, oil, and iron production to western states, or a growth
of heavy industry in midwestern and southern centers.

Toward the end of the century the uniquely important elements in Pennsylvania's history were gradually merged with
their counterparts in the rest of the nation. While the state continued a rapid economic growth after 1900, so did many other
states. In fact, all mature industrial areas have accelerated their
rates of growth in per-capita income during the twentieth century. A history of the last seventy-five years would have to be
national in scope and would be out of place in this small volume. The final chapter, therefore, summarizes only the continu-

ing relationship of Pennsylvania to the nation in business institutions and in production.

Moderately concealed, I hope, are some hypotheses regarding development. First, that it starts as a regional advance chiefly in the techniques of business, occurring in this instance along the lower Delaware River. Second, that economizing in the use of time is perhaps the most important early element in rising productivity. And third, that the process of advance becomes self-generating, each gain in efficiency calling attention to new possibilities in other directions.

I am grateful for the constant aid of the Eleutherian Mills–Hagley Foundation, both as a resource for materials and as a generator of ideas from conferences and continuing research projects in the history of the Philadelphia and Baltimore areas. The director of the library, Richmond D. Williams, has read the entire manuscript and made many helpful suggestions.

I am deeply aware of the contribution of my wife, Rosamond B. Cochran, in relieving me, up to her death, of every task in life other than reading and writing.

Radnor, Pa.   *Thomas C. Cochran*

Pennsylvania

1

Penn's Colony

PENNSYLVANIA has many claims to distinction among American states, to some people the chief one is being the home of the revolutionary congresses, the Declaration of Independence, and the Constitutional Convention; to others Pennsylvania is distinguished as the one colony that permitted all types of religious services by people of diverse nationalities and beliefs; to still others it is a region of old cities, which still show their varied cultural origins, and of beautiful green mountains, and long winding rivers. But, whether generally realized or not, Pennsylvania's greatest effects on the nation as a whole have been in business and industry. The great political documents could well have been written elsewhere, in a democratic society toleration of religious and ethnic differences would inevitably spread, but the precocious business developments that emanated from Philadelphia, the leading city of eighteenth-century America, and the later development of lumber, coal, iron, and oil depended primarily upon the unique geographical advantages of the Keystone State. Hence the chief importance of Pennsylvania in the growth of the nation comes from its first providing the essential business basis for the industrial revolution and then taking the lead in carrying it out.

As illustrated in the history of many nations, the development of wooden machinery to save labor in the manufacture of textiles is not necessarily a first step toward more general industrialization. The crucial threshold activity appears to be the manufacture of iron or, later, steel machinery for a wide range of purposes. The lathe and the roller, rather than the jenny and the loom, are more surely the precursors of mechanized industry. It was the machine shops of Chester, Philadelphia, and Wilmington (Delaware) that insured rapid industrialism in the United States. Although by 1900, because of carpets, silk, and worsteds, Pennsylvania would become the leading textile state, this was incidental to the rise of the industrially indispensable production of iron machinery powered by steam.

All economic systems are for people, and the first question, therefore, is what brought a large population to Pennsylvania in the preindustrial period? Before the advent of Europeans the fertile lands near the Delaware River were inhabited by the Lenni Lenape, the southeastern tribe of the Delaware Indians. For centuries they led a peaceful agricultural life in many small settlements that stretched up to the falls near present-day Trenton. The tribe spoke a language known as Algonquin, and by the seventeenth century it was held in a loose vassalage by the warlike Five Nations of Iroquois centered in New York.

To trade with these Indians for beaver furs, highly valued in Europe, the Dutch from New Amsterdam built Forts Nassau (1626) and Beversrede (1648) on the east bank of the Delaware. Only a few traders and soldiers occupied the forts, and there was no effort at settled farming.

Starting in 1638 Swedes and Finns made their only efforts at North American settlement by coming to the west bank of the river. At midcentury three or four hundred Swedes and Finns lived in log cabins on farms around trading posts from Fort Casimir (New Castle) northward to Christina (Wilmington), Uplands (Chester), and Tinicum and Passyunk (Philadelphia). Other than fur, tobacco was their main commodity for trading, and additional pounds of leaves were sent from Maryland and Virginia to the Swedish ships on the Delaware. The Dutch, unwilling to have the Swedes take the fur trade away from them, sent troops from New Amsterdam and easily took control of the Swedish settlements in 1655. The Dutch made a mild effort at colonization, settling New Amstel at the former Fort

Casimir, but in 1664 troops of the Duke of York made all the Dutch settlements British.

By 1680 the lower Delaware Valley had a white population of 1,500 or more, including Dutch, Swedes, Finns, and a majority of English, who had moved into West Jersey after the conquest and settled around Salem and Burlington. Meanwhile, the fur trade had become unimportant. The Lenni Lenape, decimated by European diseases and defeated by the Minquas of the Susquehanna region, had largely exhausted the beaver along the Delaware. After a total defeat by the Iroquois in 1675, even the Minquas were no longer able to supply a commercially valuable quantity of furs from the inland area.

Starting in 1682, these years of intermittent and gradual settlement gave way to a deluge of European colonists. The favorable location of the lower Delaware River and its immediate backcountry was now exploited by the unusual promotional efforts of William Penn. And these were aided between 1674 and 1715 by Germans fleeing to America from wars in the Rhineland.

William Penn (1644–1718) received Pennsylvania as a vast proprietary land grant from Charles II. Young Penn was a rare combination of influential aristocrat and active Quaker, the most extreme of the English sects that dissented from the ceremonies of the Church of England. Penn hoped to establish in America a colony where neither Quakers nor people of any other religious group would be persecuted because of their beliefs. Having lived on his father's extensive Irish estates, he was also anxious to plan a colonial economy that would avoid the bad features, which in Europe seemed to stem from centuries of unplanned growth. The royal grant was officially a repayment for money advanced to the crown by William's father, Admiral Penn, but it also illustrated the strange influence of this eloquent dissenter upon Charles II and later upon Charles's brother James II. By the year 1681 when the grant was signed, there was no large vacant area left along the seacoast from South Carolina to New Hampshire that had not been marked out as a colony; consequently, Penn received the interior land recently taken from the Dutch and the Swedes by the Duke of York. And this interior domain west of the Delaware River turned out to be the best land and the most strategic location in the colonies. Generations later it also provided the most lumber, coal, iron, and oil of any state in the Union prior to the exploitation of the northern Great Lakes and Rocky Mountain regions.

Penn thought in terms of a colony built around towns, located near enough together so that all settled farm areas would have a trading center. He also gave great thought to the laying out of Philadelphia on a gridiron pattern representative of the advanced thinking of his day about city planning. The concept of four symmetrical park areas in his rectangular city is said to be his own innovation in urban design. While Penn gave careful attention to planning the arrangement of city property, and to having substantial urban holders own nearby farmland, his interest in both helping dissident sects and raising ready money, which he always needed, quickly led him to sell large tracts of poorly defined rural acreage. For a few pence an acre, he sold thousands of unsurveyed acres to the Krefeld and Frankfort companies of Germany, as well as an indefinite amount to the Free Society of Traders in England. Later he tried to establish a price of two shillings an acre, but he never opened a land office in the colony, and buyers had to take their chances in locating their claims. With no local land office until 1732, the county courts merely confirmed titles on the basis of first use or occupancy and sought to work out compromises on boundaries. Fortunately, the Quakers were peaceful and law-abiding, as were the Dutch and Germans who settled the interior around Philadelphia, and there was still plenty of land further west. So boundary conflicts appear, in most cases, to have been resolved after much litigation but with no bloodshed.

In practice, Penn's plan for a symmetrical, rectangular, and spacious Philadelphia quickly broke down, and instead of a "greene countrie towne" stretching in an eight-block-wide band between the two rivers, as imagined by the Proprietor, the city spread far along the Delaware waterfront while penetrating inland less than a third of the way to the Schuylkill. In addition, the large blocks that were to accommodate only a few houses, each with its own garden, were soon penetrated by narrow, unsanitary alleys with small houses placed tightly together. But the large outlines of Penn's plan survived. A rectangular pattern of streets, two wide thoroughfares meeting each other in a central square, and land reserved for parks, all remained to influence both the later growth of Philadelphia and urban design across the nation.

Penn's early promotional efforts also forecast those of later generations of individual and corporate land developers. As soon as the royal grant had been completed, he began to issue promotional literature. Pamphlets measuring about eight-by-twelve inches arrested attention with large type on the first pages, followed by several more pages of description. The first pamphlet read in letters of sharply varying size: "Some account of the Province of Pennsylvania in America . . ." and sought to attract wealthy "adventurers" who would send settlers and agents, or "overseers," to the colony. Subsequent pamphlets, such as "A Letter from William Penn" to the ". . . Free Society of Traders," and newspaper advertisements brought sixty vessels loaded with thousands of settlers to the new port of Philadelphia in 1683.[1] If Penn's administrative abilities—or perhaps one should say personal interests—had equaled his literary skill as a promoter, he might have made money rather than lost it. In fact, he lost so much that, had he not been paralyzed by a stroke in 1712, he would have given the colony to Queen Anne.

The ideas and personality of William Penn are difficult to characterize; in fact, none of his contemporaries felt that they understood many of his actions. This dark-haired, rather ordinary-looking Englishman was serious and eloquent both as a preacher and a writer, apparently charming when he wanted to be but also headstrong, obstinate, and unbelievably careless in the conduct of his business affairs. Perhaps he was merely a gifted, eccentric aristocrat, rather common in a period when religious issues, *coups d'état,* and rapid changes in royal power were upsetting England. Hence, while at times he gave careful attention to the affairs of the colony, during his long life he spent only a few years in America and often seemed far out of

---

1. Letters on deposit in Rare Books Division, New York Public Library.

touch with local affairs. In the course of political and personal vicissitudes, Penn lost and regained his proprietorship, and, not surprisingly, during the period of the 1690s when Penn was always absent, the colonial assembly won more and more power from the Proprietor. He formally recognized the new relationship by granting the Charter of Privileges of 1701. In 1703 Delaware, which had been ceded to William Penn by his close friend the Duke of York in 1682, was now given permission to set up a separate council and assembly. By the time of Penn's death in 1718, the provinces were, for most purposes, self-governing democracies of local property owners administered through a single appointed governor.

In spite of Penn's eccentricities, Pennsylvania and Delaware were the only colonies planned and developed on business principles for the presumed benefit of both Proprietor and settlers. Religion was, of course, not forgotten, but there was no conflict between Quaker—or other sectarian—principles and community economic development. For the entire period from 1681 to 1775 Pennsylvania was promoted intermittently in foreign journals and booklets by two generations of Penns. As late as 1755 an advertisement by Thomas Penn in the English *Bristol Journal* offered a new suit of clothes to any handicraftsman who would "go over to the most flourishing city of Philadelphia." [2] No rich family of the mid-eighteenth century was spending comparable sums or putting forth such publicity to populate the rival seaports of Boston, Newport (Rhode Island), New York, or Charles Town (South Carolina).

Perhaps rumors of the new profits being made from land revived the interest of Penn's heirs—John, Thomas, and Richard, Anglican sons by his second wife—in closer supervision of their colony. At any rate, when their inheritance was legally assured in 1732, Thomas moved to America as deputy Proprietor for his elder brother John. Although Thomas Penn now established a local land office and validated titles drawn up since William Penn's death in 1718, the new procedures did not promise much

---

2. Carl Bridenbaugh, *Cities in Revolt: Urban Life in America, 1743–1776* (New York: Capricorn, 1964), p. 134.

improvement. No advance surveys were made, boundaries and acreage were described by the applicant; only then was a land-office survey of that particular tract made and filed. Finally a deed was transferred with six months allowed for payment. In cases of conflict, priority in any one of the stages established a claim. Landowners owed the Proprietor an annual quitrent payment of a quarter-cent per acre, but no rolls arranged by tracts were drawn up, and payment was merely a voluntary type of extra insurance of the owner's title.

John Penn, who had a double share, died before 1750, leaving it to Thomas, who now, with a three-quarter share of the proprietory interest, remained the source of ultimate authority until the American Revolution, although he appointed governors to administer the province, including John Penn, Richard's son.

Pennsylvania was immediately attractive for good farming land close to rivers, a carefully planned trade center at Philadelphia, and a businesslike representative government. Once development was vigorously under way, the gains were cumulative. From the Rhineland devastated by wars came waves of Dutch and Germans, some of whom belonged to small religious sects, and, finding surprisingly fertile farmland, these settlers urged their friends to follow. Quakers and other dissenters from England, Ireland, and Wales also wrote back, telling of their prosperity. Attracted by the settlers' glowing letters and by proprietary promotion, boatloads of immigrants continually arrived at Philadelphia. By 1700 the city probably numbered 6,000 people and the province, 20,000. The larger farms were productive enough to employ hired labor, and the port was busy enough to need more and more craftsmen and workers of many types.

The approach to Philadelphia from the ocean, however, was more difficult than to Boston or New York. Rounding Cape May at the mouth of the Delaware Bay, a sailing ship was still ninety miles by midchannel from Philadelphia, and it was seldom that a straight course could be followed. The ship usually was forced to take long tacks against the prevailing westerly winds, and many days might elapse before it reached Philadelphia. Meanwhile there was little reason for putting in at intermediate ports. The marshy shore of the bay on the Jersey side

has a number of small, fairly deep estuaries, but no navigable
rivers that reach more than a few miles into the backcountry.
The Delaware shore is also marshy and even more lacking in
rivers. At the headwaters of the bay New Castle had grown
from the trading post established by the Swedes. There, by now
in calm water, an ocean-going ship would take on a pilot to nav-
igate the winding channels of the broad Delaware River. Since
New Castle lacked both navigable inland water connections and
much population, little business could be done there. In the days
of Swedish control, the voyage would end at Upland (Chester)
about twenty miles further on, where food, implements, and Indian trade goods would be unloaded for the soldiers and fur-
traders, and, it was to be hoped, a valuable cargo of furs and
tobacco would be taken back to Europe. After the settling of
Philadelphia, a shipmaster would probably sail fifteen miles
beyond Chester to the thriving new city just above the fork of
the Delaware and the Schuylkill.

Good farming lands lay on both banks of the Delaware. The
Jersey shore, part of an ocean coastal plain, while not quite as
fertile as the hilly west bank, was steadily attracting farmers
who sent their products to the Philadelphia market. Separate in
government, West Jersey was economically a part of the expanding metropolitan region. Across the river, within a semicir-
cle bounded by distant mountains, lay the most fertile farming
lands of the northeast with Philadelphia at the center for both
local trade and export. In every direction on the Pennsylvania
side high mountains were fifty miles or more away, and most of
the intervening land was, by any standards, excellent for farming. No other protected port along the Atlantic coast had such a
combination of temperate climate, navigable rivers, and fertile
land stretching far beyond the early needs of colonial settlers.

Further to the west, ranges of Allegheny Mountains broadening in width from under fifty miles to nearly a hundred miles,
cross the state from the border with Maryland a hundred miles
west of the Susquehanna River, northeast to the meeting of the
borders of New York and New Jersey. Rising to three-thousand-
foot ridges, they often seem as even as giant waves of the sea.
At the upper end of the mountains the winding Lehigh, Dela-

ware, and Susquehanna rivers would eventually connect narrow valleys, rich in coal and iron, with the Philadelphia market, but straight west from that city the mountains offer no low passes to the continent's interior waterways. Beyond the sharp ridges of the Alleghenies lies a plateau, about 2,000 feet above sea level, which the early traveler had tortuously to attain through deep valleys and over endless hills before reaching rivers that led to the Ohio Valley, Lake Erie, or western New York. Consequently the history of the state before 1800 is chiefly that of the fertile farmlands southeast of the Allegheny Mountains.

Although population reached over 40,000 during William Penn's lifetime, there were only three counties—Chester, Philadelphia, and Bucks—running from a roughly equal frontage on the Delaware northwestward into the unsurveyed backcountry. Penn designated Chester and Bristol as the other county seats. In 1729, eleven years after his death but while his estate was still in litigation, the provincial assembly added Lancaster County. The creation of the county seat of the same name was not unconnected with the real estate operations of a politically powerful lawyer, Andrew Hamilton, an early example of the later American custom of awarding county seats to those towns with the most legislative influence.

The old counties were subdivided and new ones created between 1749 and the Revolution, until all the land up to. and including some of the mountain area was divided into such units. Early counties had a courthouse town at the center of an area small enough so that no one would have to travel more than about a dozen miles to do his county business.

It is estimated that at the beginning of the Revolution there were some 300,000 people in the colony, with Germans, Scotch-Irish, and other British people present in about equal numbers. From early days Philadelphia was regarded as the best colonial port to unload the many people who had "indentured" their services for a number of years in exchange for their passage to America. Perhaps two-thirds of the immigrants to Pennsylvania had come under indenture, particularly the Scotch-Irish from impoverished Ulster. Latecomers from the latter group who arrived from 1717 on found cheap land only in the backcountry, where some of their farms were in the deep valleys of the Alleghenies. Meanwhile German immigration had virtually ended in 1755. In spite of the greatest mixture of nationalities of any population south of Quebec, the colony was not made up of sharply defined ethnic regions. People of all nationalities had tended to move west on an individual basis, sometimes establishing ethnic communities but not entire counties.

As far west as the first ranges of the mountains latecomers were at no great economic disadvantage. Productivity varied somewhat with the fertility of the soil, but not on an east-west basis. Land across the Susquehanna was often equal to the best in Chester County or Lancaster County, and if Philadelphia was far away, Maryland ports were nearer, and more accessible after a road was opened to Chesapeake Bay in 1743. Geographer James Lemon thinks the variation in fertility between areas was slight, and production depended mainly on the intensity of work by the farmer.[3] Everywhere in the colonial period cultivation was superficial. The Lancaster County German sects such as the Amish and Mennonites became famous as exceptionally good farmers, but Lemon does not find this superiority borne out by the available early records. It seems likely that they became widely known by staying on the same land generation after generation—a great exception in America—preserving their quaint social customs, and maintaining the fertility of the limestone soil by using familiar mid-eighteenth-century German agricultural practices.

Except for these "Pennsylvania Dutch," Swiss, and other German sectarians, farmers bought and sold land in hopes of profit, and younger men continually moved to find better opportunities. Migration in quest of profit and ready changes in occupation differentiated America from old and regulated Europe and gave the whole colonial society an atmosphere of devotion to business.

By the mid-eighteenth century many landowners were holding acreages for their increasing value and meanwhile renting to

---

3. James T. Lemon, *The Best Poor Man's Country: A Geographical Study of Early Southern Pennsylvania* (Baltimore: Johns Hopkins University Press, 1972), p. 224.

both farming and business tenants. In 1750, in Chester County, 27 percent of the farmers were tenants, and in Lancaster County to the west, 36 percent. The cities, of course, ran higher in tenancy; Lancaster had 41 percent and Germantown, 56 percent. In the towns landowners whose properties fronted a main street usually built and rented small buildings for stores and workshops. Many in-town properties represented a sort of agribusiness combination, on which a retailer or craftsman both had his shop and cultivated an adjoining plot too small for commercial farming.

While most backcountry crafts were aimed at supplying local needs for wood, flour, leather goods, or farm implements, iron production for the Philadelphia market had, by its nature, to be a country industry. A blast furnace for smelting iron required not only a deposit of ore near the surface, but a nearby limestone quarry and thousands of acres of woodland. Fueled by charcoal made from wood, an average eighteenth-century furnace, using four hundred bushels of charcoal per ton of iron, would consume six thousand cords of wood per year. Consequently, iron "plantations" that supplied their own wood ran from five thousand to ten thousand acres. Some with smaller acreages, such as Mt. Joy at Valley Forge, had to buy wood. In addition, the self-sufficient plantation, which was the rule, had small houses for the workers and their families who cultivated surrounding fields to raise their food. Except for the smoke and glare of furnaces or the banging of hammers at the forges, the plantation resembled a feudal manor with its owner's mansion and surrounding village of dependent—often slave or indentured—workers. Even though in most cases the local manager shared ownership with Philadelphia merchants, the iron plantation houses included some of the most elaborate country dwellings of the early period.

Heating with charcoal and adding plentiful local limestone broke down, or smelted, the ore, and the heavy liquid iron drawn from the bottom of the furnace was poured into hollows made of clay, sand, and loam in the form of rectangular "pigs." To be useful to a blacksmith or toolmaker, the pigs had to be reshaped into thin strips or bars, and this was done by re-heating and hammering in a forge. The forge used much less wood than the charcoal smelter, but it required waterpower to run the hammer; hence furnaces and forges might be in different places, although it was obviously more efficient to have the operations together.

German and Welsh settlers were familiar with locating iron ore, and both veins and surface deposits were soon discovered in much of southern and central Pennsylvania. Before 1720 iron plantations had been started in the Schuylkill Valley with capital supplied from Philadelphia. The most important complete iron works of this period was located about fifty miles north of Philadelphia, where a mill creek flowed into the Delaware River. Eight leading merchants and lawyers of Philadelphia, including James Logan, secretary of the colony; William Allen, later Pennsylvania's chief justice; and Anthony Morris; put up the money as partners to start this Durham works in 1729. With practically unbroken surrounding forest, a stream that powered three forges, and relatively cheap transportation down the Delaware, the works was one of the most successful of the early colonial period. By the time of the Revolution, iron was being made on many streams east of the Susquehanna. The pig or forged iron reaching Philadelphia was made into steel (contrary to imperial regulations against finished iron products that might compete with those of Britain), tin plate, nails, and tools for home consumption, and the surplus crude iron was exported to Britain.

The port of Philadelphia throve more than all others because it dominated this very large and prosperous backcountry. About thirty miles was the extreme limit for a day's drive with a loaded wagon over dirt roads. And the condition of the roads grew worse as travel grew heavier. Many farmers, probably most within the thirty-mile range, preferred to buy and sell in the metropolis rather than at nearer but small county towns such as Chester or Bristol, both a little less than twenty miles away from the provincial center. In fact, no large boroughs, other than the semisuburban manufacturing center of Germantown, developed within fifty miles of Philadelphia. Rather than trade at a local county town, some people living more than thirty miles away were willing to take a couple of days to reach the port. If they were prosperous, they might eat and sleep in one of the inns or taverns that dotted the main roads. But it was not hard to live for a few days in the farm wagon.

All of this movement runs counter to old conceptions that overland trade in grain, for example, was impossible for more than fifteen or twenty miles. What the early economic calculators neglected was the fact that there were times of the year, particularly right after harvest, when the farmer had nothing to do immediately beyond chores, which could be carried on by his family. The horse or horses would eat little more on the road than at home. Consequently, a four- or five-day round trip to the city, with all supplies carried from home, cost little beyond wear and tear on the wagon. And, in addition, the farmer might enjoy his semiannual visit to the source of information and exotic excitement.

Only Germantown seems to have thrived, within five miles of downtown Philadelphia, by developing industries supplementary to those at the center, as well as being a convenient stop for drivers coming to Philadelphia from the northwest. One historian writes: "It was craft and processing raised to a surprisingly complex and sophisticated level, rather than commerce or trade, which formed the backbone of the economic system of Germantown, and made it unique among Pennsylvania towns." [4] Built on high bluffs above the Schuylkill, it was less humid than Philadelphia in hot weather and hence became a resort, with the usual summer rentals and tourist trade. Local makers of fine saddles, fancy cloth, or carriages could sell some of their products at retail to prosperous people from "the city."

At the start William Penn had encouraged road building by awarding extra grants of land. In 1686 the colonial council ruled that road construction was county business, but from 1700 on, it had assisted king's or queen's highways between major places, such as from Philadelphia south to Chester (1706) and north on

4. Stephanie Grauman Wolf, *An Urban Village: Population, Community and Family Structure in Germantown, Pennsylvania* (Princeton: Princeton University Press, 1976), p. 102.

Old York Road (1711). Such highways were merely strips fifty feet wide with stumps and boulders removed. Their condition varied with the heaviness of traffic and the time of year, but was generally bad.

The major request for a road in the colonial period was one sent to the assembly in 1730 by the new county seat of Lancaster, to connect it with Philadelphia nearly seventy miles away. The request was granted in 1733, and the Great Conestoga Road was completed in 1741. It marked the colony's first major effort at interior development and would ultimately, in 1758, be a link on the Pennsylvania road to Pittsburgh. In 1736 a king's highway was started from Easton and Allentown to Reading. By the late colonial period three stagecoach lines ran regularly between New York and Philadelphia, taking about three days each way.

Public transportation in the form of Conestoga freight wagons drawn by up to six horses was available after midcentury on the king's highways. Leather goods, clocks, fancy woodcarving, and pig or bar iron could stand the cost and were moved to Philadelphia by wagon from fifty or sixty miles away. By that time highways fanned out from Philadelphia in all directions, and before the Revolution traffic was said to be so heavy on the Great Conestoga Road to Lancaster that a rule of passing to the right had to be enforced, perhaps because drivers moved all over the road trying to avoid deep holes and ruts. In addition to the incredibly bad surface and unbridged streams, an annoyance to truckers was the large number of cattle or hogs being driven to the Philadelphia market from deep in the backcountry, sometimes in large herds put together by several farmers and taken over by a professional drover acting as a middleman. So country products of all kinds—wheat, corn, liquor, flour, meat, iron, and flax—reached Philadelphia in quantities that helped supply other parts of the world.

Philadelphia's good fortune in the timing of its settlement applied to overseas trade as well as to immigrants. In the early eighteenth century, West Indies trade grew rapidly and required grain, meat, and lumber. Not only was Philadelphia the best supplier of these, it was the easiest major port to reach from the Caribbean. After 1750, when Maryland and Virginia shifted from tobacco to more wheat growing and cattle raising, and better roads brought products from west of the Susquehanna River, Philadelphia began to face competition, but its market was still much bigger than any to the south.

Growth of the colony beyond the Susquehanna River or on the upper reaches of the Delaware was contingent upon Indian policy as well as on transportation. Until 1732 an ill-defined policy of buying land from the few remaining Delawares, when the latter particularly needed money for rum or other trade goods, had been pursued without careful understanding between the two sides. The white officials believed they were buying outright; often the Indian chiefs, who lacked the concept of private land titles, thought that they were selling the mutual use of the areas.

Advised by the long-time secretary of the colony, James Logan, Thomas Penn considered the whole Indian situation in broad terms. The territory of the Iroquois or Five Nations in New York formed a valuable protective zone against the French in Canada. Since the weak and peaceable Delawares were vassals of the Iroquois, the Pennsylvania Indian policy should be chiefly directed to friendship with the powerful Five Nations. For this purpose John Schickellamy, an English-speaking Iroquois, and Conrad Weiser, a German who had been admitted as a youth to the Mohawk tribe of the Iroquois federation, were of great use as negotiators. In 1736 all the Iroquois chiefs participated in a treaty ceding to Pennsylvania the southeastern region and a strip west of the Delaware River up to the fork with the Lehigh. The strip was to be as wide as a man could walk in a day, but trained runners went twice as far as the Indians expected. This tricky interpretation of the "the Walking Purchase," by the agents of the colony permanently alienated the Delawares. The Indian view that they had been cheated was supported by powerful Pennsylvania Quakers. Nevertheless, the Iroquois ceded additional land further west at the Treaty of Lancaster in 1844.

The most serious breakdown in Indian relations occurred in the decade after 1754, when the Delawares and their Quaker friends demanded reparations for the excessive area claimed under the "Walking Purchase." This prevented proper tribal unanimity on a new general agreement for cession of western land below a line from Sunbury to Warren on the Allegheny River. But more important was the failure of the province to build and garrison western forts that could protect both whites and Indians from French inroads south of Lake Erie, or to give promised supplies to the Indians. The Anglican Proprietor Thomas Penn was willing to contribute half the cost of fortifications, but the Quaker-dominated assembly would not raise troops or money unless the Penns allowed their proprietory land to be taxed for the first time. Hence the western Pennsylvania Indians, without aid from Philadelphia, were forced to accept the French as allies. The situation was furthered complicated by Virginia's claim to western Pennsylvania.

A minor engagement in 1755 between Virginia militia and French troops in Pennsylvania started a European war. The government in London sent Major General Edward Braddock with two regiments of regulars to demolish the French positions from Fort Duquesne at the Forks of the Ohio to Presque Isle at present-day Erie. Proceeding through Virginia and up the Monongahela River into Pennsylvania, Braddock's advance force was badly defeated and he was killed by French and Indian troops. The colonel next in command withdrew the entire British force to Philadelphia, leaving the rest of the province without protection from bands of Delawares and other Indians seeking vengeance for indignities suffered since 1737. By October of 1755 it was said that practically no white settlers remained west of the Susquehanna, and no farm beyond the outskirts of Philadelphia was really safe.

The raids had lasting repercussions on provincial politics. The Quakers in the assembly split into a "war" faction that voted money for forts and a "principled" group whose abstention from voting allowed the defense measure to pass. In the elections of 1756 only ten Quakers were returned to the assembly and their seventy-five-year political control of the province came to an end.

A chain of provincial forts and stockades was built that same year, all the way from Easton on the Delaware to Lewistown in the western mountains. The next year a British army under Brigadier General John Forbes was sent by the new prime minister, William Pitt, and the western situation again changed dramatically. Carefully building a supply road from Bedford to just east of Pittsburgh, Forbes moved an irresistible force of 5,000 British and American troops westward in 1758. The French chose not to fight and demolished their forts as they retreated. Forced always to side with those in control, the local Indians again became allies of the British, and Fort Pitt replaced the former Fort Duquesne at the Forks of the Ohio.

The economic growth of the western part of the colony, however, was still held back by a combination of military and political problems. White frontiersmen, calling themselves Paxton Boys, attacked Indian settlements, murdering whole families and, in 1763, brought on a reprisal by a large force from Canada under Ottawa Chief Pontiac. His army was defeated by the experienced British Colonel Henry Bouquet at Bushy Run near Fort Pitt; but meanwhile the government in London cast doubt on the legality of all western settlements. The rethinking of imperial problems that came with British victory in the Seven Years (French and Indian) War convinced the cabinet that settlement should be kept more compact and closer to the coast. The resulting Royal Proclamation of 1763 restricted settlement and land ownership to a line along the watershed between rivers that ultimately reached the Atlantic Ocean and those flowing toward the Mississippi Valley, and also required licenses for Indian trade. Therefore, although settlement in the later Pittsburgh-Erie-Warren areas became relatively safe once more, it was now illegal.

But in the 1760s these nearly isolated areas had relatively little economic effect on the province east of the mountains. Aided by favorable factors of fertile land, generally sober, industrious people, representative government, fine natural resources, and profitable overseas trade, by 1770 Pennsylvania led the American colonies in manufacturing and in the size and wealth of its major seaport. The supremacy of Philadelphia in manufacturing would last for three-quarters of a century, decades after New York had taken the lead in foreign trade. The unusual self-sufficiency of the total Pennsylvania economy would still be evident in the twentieth century.

2

Colonial Business and the War for Independence

*T*HE growth of Pennsylvania settlements in area, population, and wealth provide background for a closer look at the offices and shops of the province to see how businessmen were meeting their practical problems. Instead of scanning the whole colony, we may concentrate on the great port of Philadelphia and its immediate backcountry since, except for import and export, the same general types of business were being conducted in Lancaster, Reading, Bristol, and many smaller centers.

Yet, each city had its particular business attitudes, or climate. Travelers coming to Philadelphia were uniformly impressed with the sober, businesslike atmosphere of the city and its people. Undoubtedly the early Quaker influence accounted for some of the sobriety, but the Quakers, though unusually devoted to business pursuits, soon became a minority of the population. Families lectured their children on thrift, frugality, and avoidance of debt, while preachers of all denominations repeated these admonitions on Sundays and added warnings against licentious behavior and wasting God's time. The annual meetings of the combined New Jersey and Pennsylvania Quakers were regularly used for the exchange of business information. Both the indentured immigrants, working off their fare from Europe, and the apprentices bound out by their parents had to learn the ways of trade.

Since no guild regulations or class distinctions excluded new-comers from starting any kind of a business, the society was highly competitive. Immigrants from different parts of Europe brought skills that were more and more advanced, and then in-novated still further as they applied them in the new environ-ment, so that local artisans could not rely for long on outmoded traditional practices. In a society expanding in every direction it was hard for masters to keep their journeymen, merchants to keep their clerks, or fathers to keep their children devoted to a family enterprise.

While individual vigor and initiative flourished in such an en-vironment, competition was almost impossible with less expen-sive British and European products made by highly skilled but poorly paid spinners, weavers, grinders, and polishers. Con-sequently, the colonies continued to import sheetings, table linen, cambrics, sail cloth, and cutlery, as well as luxuries in clothing and household decoration. Pennsylvanians could have lived without imports, but they would have had to give up many of the amenities of life, and would have had to cultivate bees and maple trees for sugar.

The key figure in foreign trade was the merchant, who col-lected in his waterfront warehouse the grains, salt meat, lumber, and iron of the backcountry, exchanging them for foreign manu-factures, wine, tea, sugar, and molasses. The merchant, in car-rying on his activities, became involved in most of the business of the city and the province, doing alone the work of a dozen later specialists, ranging from those in finance to retail trade.

Robert Morris and Barnard Gratz illustrate two typical ways of entering upon a mercantile career. Both had fathers in wholesale trade, but Morris's father was a rather obscure Eng-lish tobacco agent at Oxford, Maryland. In the late 1740s he sent his thirteen-year-old, English-bred son to an academy in Philadelphia, under the care of a friend who was able to obtain for the genial and attractive young Morris an apprenticeship in the important office of Charles Willing and Son. At the end of Robert's apprenticeship, he was hired by the firm and, in spite of his youth, was trusted as a supercargo (business agent) on voyages to the West Indies. In 1754 after the death of Charles Willing, Morris was invited by Willing's son Thomas to enter into a partnership. Since Morris could not have had any large capital, the invitation must have come because the English-educated Thomas—"Old Square Toes," as he was later nick-named by his friends—recognized that Robert Morris was becoming a congenial and extraordinarily able businessman.

The rise of Morris had depended on the fortunate influence of a family friend combined with his own background and personality needed to make the most of his opportunities. Barnard Gratz's success during about the same years illustrates the more usual path, based on important European family connections and money as well as ability. It was also part of a normal pattern that Barnard's initial training was in Europe and England and that he came to America with a small capital and an established connection with Philadelphia merchant David Franks of Franks and Simon. After various business ventures with Franks, including contracting for the British army in the French and Indian War, Barnard Gratz formed a partnership in the late 1760s with his younger brother Michael. For the next generation B. & M. Gratz were among the leading merchants of Philadelphia.

These two methods of entering the top mercantile ranks also illustrate the religious divisions in the merchant community between Jews, Quakers, and other Protestants, mostly Anglicans. The Quakers, particularly, had a wide business network all over the western world and whenever possible did business with each other. Jewish merchants such as Gratz, belonging to a much smaller colonial group than the Quakers, favored trading with members of their own faith, although they did not in any way discourage business from men of other beliefs. Willing and Morris did not expect much business from either of these closely knit religious groups, but in the largest part of world of trade commercial activities were not affected by religious beliefs.

From 1700 to 1763, the British Empire was at war about half the time, and while normal American trade to the West Indies and Europe was made more hazardous, lucrative army and navy contracts for supplies and repairs brought sterling currency into the hands of merchants who normally only saw pounds as notations of payment due to their British correspondents. During the French and Indian War, Franks and Simon, perhaps because the latter was in Lancaster, received £750,000 in British army contracts.

Because of both the imperial navigation acts and the supremacy of Britain in many types of manufacture, credit with British merchants was almost an essential of success for colonists engaged in foreign trade. The standing of a Philadelphia house depended greatly on its reputation in England for caution, good judgment, and reliable settlement of accounts. Normally accounts were liquidated once or twice a year by sending wheat, flour, timber, and iron from Pennsylvania, plus goods from the West Indies or Continental Europe acquired in the course of roundabout voyages. Since Pennsylvania products often sold for sterling or Spanish dollars in the West Indies, thus providing a cash basis for paying some British exporters of manufactures, the Philadelphia merchants had the best credit in the colonies.

Even in this port, however, specie was quickly drained away to pay accounts in Bristol, Liverpool, London, or Glasgow, and the local market was left short of money for routine business. Because of fewer merchants with access to specie, inland trade centers suffered even more severely. To meet this problem in 1723 the Pennsylvania assembly with the approval of William Keith, governor during the litigation of the Penn estate, authorized an issue of paper currency backed by real estate mortgages or silver plate. This type of plan is sometimes referred to as a land bank. Loan offices were opened, in which the state agents would evaluate the security and lend on mortgages, paying the borrower in notes of from one shilling to one pound. In this first bill £45,000 in eight-year mortgages was authorized, and subsequent laws added to the total amount and extended mortgages to sixteen years. By 1740 about £80,000 was in circulation.

The Pennsylvania system was carefully run, and while merchants preferred specie, the local currency always passed at better than 70 and sometimes at 90 percent of its face value in terms of British sterling. Thomas Penn disapproved of continued issue, but the king accepted £5,000 in Pennsylvania currency for military purposes in 1744. Ultimately, badly run currencies, particularly in the New England colonies, caused local inflation and led Parliament in 1764 to ban further issues, but, on the whole, paper money stimulated the growth of business in the colonies. In addition, Pennsylvanians received valuable experience that, after independence, equipped them to be leaders in commercial banking.

In the mature colony of the mid-eighteenth century, internal trade was conducted by both barter and cash. Farmers bringing grain to large millers along the tributaries of the Delaware would often be paid in cash. So would the boatmen who took the flour by shallop—a small sailing vessel—from the miller to the exporter in Philadelphia. The exporter was the source of the money that flowed inland in this manner. Specie or colonial currency would return to Philadelphia as millers, boatmen, shopkeepers, and farmers came to buy in the central urban market.

Farmers not close to water transport might find it best to have their wheat ground at a local mill and then take the produce to Philadelphia in their own wagons. If the buyers from the interior dealt chiefly with a single merchant, they might use the same type of "bookkeeping" barter carried on by the importer with his British correspondents. Wagons full of flour, with perhaps a cow or calf trailing behind, would come to the narrow shops of Philadelphia merchants on Front near Market Street, and after some haggling the merchants would give the farmer or inland shopkeeper a credit of so many pounds, shillings, and pence on his books. The flour would be stored awaiting export or sold to retailers, and the cattle turned over to a butcher selling in the High Street market. Some of the meat would be salted and then sold by the butcher to an exporter. The backcountry man might take home cloth, cutting implements, and other farm or household equipment made by local or British master craftsmen, leaving either a small debt or credit balance with the merchant. At no time had much money changed hands. To have a customer somewhat in debt assured the merchant of continuing patronage. If such obligations became large, the merchant might ask that they be covered by a mortgage on the debtor's real estate.

Good judgment of how much credit to extend to various buyers was, and has always remained, one of the requirements of success in wholesale trade. Aided by false letters of recommendation, swindlers operated in the colonial period with as much success as in later years. Coming to Philadelphia in 1760 presumably to start a mercantile house, one John White secured enough credit to build and stock a ship on which he and his wife sailed away for parts unknown. Such experiences led a merchant to observe that colonial commerce floated on an ocean of skepticism, and honesty was the most sought-for quality in distant correspondents. Usually fraud was less intentional and less dramatic than in the case of John White. The poorly located or inept storekeeper, finding his debts to several merchants too large to repay, would simply disappear into the backcountry. Without any initial intention of deceit some merchants used the Revolutionary situation to avoid paying their debts to British merchants, but this was less true of Pennsylvanians than of the businessmen in some of the deeply indebted colonies, such as Virginia.

The West Indies trade aided greatly in keeping Philadelphia merchants out of long-term debt to their British correspondents. The Caribbean islands acquired specie from selling sugar and molasses to Europe, and they needed the food—available in the largest volume and at the lowest prices—from the Philadelphia backcountry. Cut timber for building and ready-made furniture often accompanied the flour and salt meat on outward voyages. The ships, less costly than North Atlantic vessels, brought back legal kegs of molasses from the British possessions and illegal ones from the Dutch, French, and Spanish islands, together with specie, usually in Spanish dollars. Port and Madeira wine from Spain might also be bought illegally. Smuggling did not usually mean landing at night on the shore of a lonely Jersey inlet, but merely the substitution of false bills of lading, indicating that the cargo had come from British islands. The not-too-curious customs officials maintained a good standard of living from the moderate gratuities involved.

Merchants owned almost all the ocean-going vessels, important houses might own several; Willing and Morris, while still a medium-sized firm, owned three, and small merchants often joined together in building and operating ships. Since all ocean trips were somewhat hazardous, there was an advantage in spreading risks through joint ownership. Long voyages to the Mediterranean, Britain, and return, often lasting half a year or more, might be set up as separate partnerships in which five or six houses bought shares in a full-rigged ship. In contrast, profitable West Indies voyages might be completed in a couple of months in schooners of only one to two hundred tons. In the early 1770s Philadelphians owned more than 135 ships but only 84 horse-drawn carriages.

Marine insurance was also handled co-operatively. A merchant wanting insurers for a voyage would place a sheet describing vessel, goods, and destination on a special table in Philadelphia's London Coffee House, where interested businessmen would sign to accept shares of the risk at the specified premium rate. Toward the end of the colonial period merchants such as Thomas Wharton on Carpenter's Wharf, or Thomas Willing across the street, advertised their readiness to arrange for marine insurance. Often, however, insurance was arranged by a merchant's correspondent in London, where the process was more expeditious and probably more reliable.

Having ties to the great London money market, which by the end of the colonial period was superseding Amsterdam as the world's center of trade and finance, the wealthy Philadelphia merchant served as an all-purpose financier. He lent on mortgages, carried credits on his books (deposits) at interest, bought British government securities for customers, and invested personally or through syndicates in all forms of local enterprise. Robert Morris did so much banking that he was trying to charter a special company when the Revolution intervened. Groups of Philadelphia merchants not only financed big enterprises such as iron plantations and shipyards, but also became silent partners in the activities of builders, publishers, and other craftsmen. Always the successful merchant was on prowl for promising real estate. Ocean voyages were risky, and sons might lack the business abilities of fathers, but urban property seemed a sure basis for a permanent family fortune.

The Treaty of Paris, which ended the French and Indian War in 1763, opened the Ohio Valley to the fur trade. Philadelphia firms such as David Franks & Company, Simon and Levy, and Baynton, Wharton and Morgan, quickly became active in this business. In 1766 the latter firm dispatched a train of six hundred packhorses carrying £50,000 worth of trade goods to Pittsburgh, where it was put on boats for trade all the way to the Mississippi. The size of the party illustrates the need for many men to protect both the trinkets and the furs from red or white marauders. It also illustrates the early beginning of lively trade between Philadelphia and Pittsburgh.

Before the French and Indian War the Front Street offices of even the leading merchants were far from impressive. The usual two-and-a-half-story building, including living quarters, was about twenty by twenty-five feet plus a kitchen wing. The office, which took up about half the first floor, was a mixture of high desks, stools, samples, and actual stocks of some specially valuable goods. Proprietors or partners together with a clerk who knew bookkeeping and a servant or apprentice carried on the business. As the volume of trade increased in the 1750s, the leading merchants built homes on the nearby streets and devoted Front Street more and more exclusively to business, but as late as the mid-1780s the prosperous dealer in foreign exchange Haym Salomon was still living over his Front Street office.

In a day with no screens and vast squadrons of mosquitoes from the nearby marshes, a high and dry country seat was usually the earliest addition to the housing of the prosperous businessman. Along the rising banks of the Schuylkill or Wissa-hickon, or in the hills of Delaware County, his family could spend much of the year. Absence of the family also left the entrepreneur time during the week to frequent the coffee houses, which became more and more specialized exchanges for goods, real estate, and securities. The merchant's life was seldom a hurried one. Between the dispatch or reception of shipments, there were many days or weeks during which the clerk could run the office while the proprietor inspected his real estate holdings or lived the life of a country gentleman.

While "merchant" was the most prestigious business occupation, and many men who were only small operators in imports and exports listed themselves on the tax rolls under this title, the great majority of businessmen were retailers, master craftsmen, and artisans, including many in the building trades. Philadelphia was a city of individual entrepreneurs in single shops. Hired laborers, indentured servants, and slaves made up less than a quarter of the population, with seamen the largest single segment of the wage earners.

High Street and the cross streets as far as Fifth or Sixth were lined by a haphazard mixture of stores, bakeries, workshops, and houses, although as time went on there began to be some special areas for luxury goods such as silver and fine furniture. Rich and poor alike patronized the many bakeries and grocery stores. The tailors, shoemakers (cordwainers), woodworkers (joiners), and other craftsmen worked in their shops fronting the street and interrupted their tasks to write down new orders. Some had an apprentice or a family member to help, but real manufacturing establishments were rare. Spinning and weaving of wool and flax were done chiefly at home in both the city and the surrounding countryside.

Within a particular type of manufacture there was little division of labor by specialization or limitation of individual tasks, such as only cutting leather for shoe soles or cloth for garments. Ladies' dresses were made largely at home by housewives, daughters, or hired seamstresses. The exceptions to the small shop were a very few shipyards, ropewalks, brick kilns, iron works, candle factories, and a few other centralized plants, most of whose product was sold to other businessmen for use or distribution.

The whole complex of this "great city" of the late colonial days, which was claimed probably erroneously to be the second largest in the Empire, included some seven thousand houses in a crescent-shaped area. The Delaware River curved along the inside of the crescent, which had an outer edge beginning below South Street, reached maximum width at Market and Seventh, and rounded back to the river above Vine Street. Thus the statehouse that was to play such a prominent role in creating the new nation was relatively far uptown, Washington Square—the nearest of William Penn's four parks—was the potter's field, and wealthy citizens driving along High Street and Germantown or Chester pikes to their country seats were in the suburbs well before they reached Penn's proposed central square, the site of present-day city hall.

Of the professional groups, lawyers began to be important only in the 1730s, but William Allen, chief justice of the provincial court, was one of the most influential men in the middle years of the century, as was Quaker lawyer John Dickinson in the decade before the Revolution. Physicians, although taught by apprenticeship, nevertheless commanded customary social respect. Printers were a business group of much greater importance then than in later years. Commanding all aspects of mass communication from papermaking to newspaper and book publishing, some printers were more than equivalent to present-day publishers in both business and social influence. Philadelphia, as became the great business center of the colonies, had for over sixty years one of the chief printer-publishers of the world, Benjamin Franklin.

When the seventeen-year-old Franklin arrived in Philadelphia in 1723, colonial newspaper publishing was in its infancy. The local *American Weekly Mercury,* the earliest newspaper in the middle colonies and third on the continent, had been started by Andrew Bradford at the end of 1719. The fourth colonial paper, the *New England Courant,* had been started by Franklin's brother James in Boston in 1721. Young Ben, apprenticed to his brother, had gained valuable experience in editing the *Courant.* Leaving Boston because he did not get on with his brother, the newly released apprentice secured employment as a journeyman with Samuel Keimer, one of the two Philadelphia printers. Shortly thereafter, one of Franklin's brothers-in-law, a ship's captain, called the boy to the attention of Governor Keith, a man of great ambitions, who was anxious to set up a better printer in Philadelphia.

Promising him all the necessary financial support for a new shop, Keith dispatched Franklin to England to buy type and see the most up-to-date methods of printing. But when Franklin reached London, no gubernatorial money was provided, a failure not uncommon in dealings with Keith. Some two years later, after working at printing and giving swimming lessons to young aristocrats, Franklin returned to Philadelphia as the clerk of a Quaker merchant with whom he had cultivated a warm friendship. The merchant died within a year, and Franklin, finding no opening for a bookkeeper, in 1727 returned to printing with his former employer. Extremely hard work and his ability at both business and making friends, together with the general ineptness of Keimer, helped Franklin to become the sole proprietor by 1730 of the three-year-old *Pennsylvania Gazette* and its print shop.

From this time on, Franklin quickly became the rare combination of an intellectual, civic, and business leader. His first step toward fame, in fact, preceded the acquisition from Keimer of the *Pennsylvania Gazette*. Franklin formed the Junto, a club of aspiring young men who were interested in reading, good conversation, and their mutual business advancement, a more intellectual version of a twentieth-century service club, such as Rotary or Kiwanis. One of its first services was to start a circulating library, initially for the members of the club, but soon—as the Library Company of Philadelphia—open to all subscribers.

Franklin combined keen intellectual penetration and great energy with an understanding of public relations and the inevitable community character of urban problems and enterprises. He realized that business growth required police and fire protection, as well as provisions for public health and education, and that the only way to secure these advantages from an indifferent proprietory government was through private organizing activity. Each of these services in Philadelphia was largely the creation of Franklin. Volunteer fire companies began in the 1740s with his group named the Union; and a dozen years later (1752) he took the lead in organizing the Philadelphia Contributorship for Insuring Houses Against Loss by Fire, called, because of the design of its seal, the Hand in Hand. In the same decade he led in establishing the College of Philadelphia (the University of Pennsylvania) and the city hospital (Pennsylvania General Hospital).

Meanwhile, Franklin's printing enterprises prospered greatly. From 1732 to 1758, in *Poor Richard's Almanac,* edited under his pseudonym, Richard Saunders, he was, according to historian Carl Becker, annually "pilfering the world's store of aphorisms, and adapting them to the circumstances and understanding of the poor." [1] With a circulation that soon reached 10,000, the *Almanac* became, next to the Bible, the most universally seen book in the colonies. By 1748 Franklin ended his office work, leaving the daily tasks to his business-minded wife, Deborah, and a managing partner David Hall. Under their guidance the *Gazette* continued until the end of the colonial period to maintain a leading position among the five Philadelphia papers.

Meanwhile Franklin was pursuing a career in politics and an avocation in science that are only of indirect interest to our economic study. Yet his "passion for improvement" was manifest in his activities as deputy postmaster general of Philadelphia from 1737 to 1753 and in sharing with William Hunter the same post for all the colonies from 1754 to 1774. He not only continually speeded up the mails, a primary service to business in which time was almost universally one of the chief costs, but he made the post office pay! He also worked for a reform of the colony's tax system that would make the proprietory lands subject to levies, and in 1760 he succeeded insofar as the Penns' improved property was concerned. Ironically Franklin, a Deist, or his lieutenants led the antiproprietory Quaker group in the assembly.

Franklin's achievements typified the increasing specialization of business functions in fast-growing Philadelphia. The fire insurance company, an employment agency, which gave particular aid to the hordes of immigrants, merchants specializing in insuring marine risks, a steel mill (illegal by British regulation), and stage boats on the Delaware were all parts of a combination of business facilities not equaled elsewhere in the colonies. From the early 1750s until the Revolution the city enjoyed an almost continuous boom broken only by a few years of recession in the mid-1760s. During this time the immigrants flooding

1. Dictionary of American Biography, 11 vols. (New York: Scribner's, 1946) 5:587.

into the backcountry, not only from Europe but from New England and New York, poured larger and larger supplies of farm products into the Philadelphia market. Bigger and more mechanized flour mills on the Brandywine, Schuylkill, and Wissahickon converted country wheat into flour for local consumption and export. In 1774 Philadelphia shipped flour worth £720,000 and maintained a favorable over-all trade balance of £100,000.

As such figures indicate, the city was on the verge of becoming the one center in the colonies which could export capital for large projects. The five hundred or so business leaders who ran the city and the colony were said to be "canal mad," with plans under way to connect the Schuylkill and the Susquehanna, as well as Delaware Bay and Chesapeake Bay. When interrupted by the war, the merchants had also plans to start a joint stock bank, and, most grandiose of all, to secure a proprietory type grant to a corporation for a new western colony, Vandalia. In all, it seems probable that the war with Britain delayed by a decade or more a quantum jump in business organization in Philadelphia. But perhaps the growth of so economically mature a colony in the old empire would ultimately have led to trouble had there been no Boston Tea Party.

In fact, the North American colonies with a population, exclusive of Canada, almost half that of Britain, with a prodigious rate of growth in population, and with a feeling of belonging to a new and unique society were inevitably going to present critical imperial problems. From 1763 on, British ministers precipitated the trouble by efforts at regulation and taxation. In the ensuing dozen years of intermittent quarrels, however, Pennsylvanians played more the roles of mediators than leaders of resistance. Benjamin Franklin and Robert Morris, the two most famous Pennsylvanians of the Revolutionary period, typified peaceful, practical Philadelphians seeking solutions for difficulties rather than fiery advocates of American rights, such as Samuel Adams and Patrick Henry.

The cabinet of Prime Minister George Grenville, who came to office in 1763, thought that the colonies should bear a fair share of the annual cost of imperial defense, which up to this time they had done only on an occasional voluntary basis. For this purpose, in 1764, tariff duties to raise revenue were placed on colonial imports such as sugar, molasses, wine, coffee, silk, and other goods, and new efforts were made to prevent smuggling. When the new customs duties failed to produce satisfactory revenue, a stamp tax on legal documents, customs manifests, and newspapers was added in 1765. The colonial reaction to this "internal" tax was surprisingly violent and brought into question the right of Parliament to levy taxes on his Majesty's subjects overseas.

Pennsylvania's position in the ensuing years of quarrels and resistance to parliamentary taxation was unique in several ways. While Quakers were now a rather small minority of the population of Pennsylvania, they were among the wealthy and responsible leaders of the eastern area. Most of them were opposed to measures that might lead to violence of any type. There was also a large German population in the backcountry that was not easily aroused over matters of British politics. But most important of all, at the start of the trouble was the strength of antiproprietory feeling in the province. Franklin, serving in London as the colonial agent and representing the antiproprietory majority in the provincial assembly, hoped the Grenville ministry might end the proprietorship and make Pennsylvania a royal colony with the right to tax the proprietory lands.

Consequently Franklin, not wanting to alienate Grenville on the proprietory issue, supported the British tax policies from 1763 to 1765. In not objecting to the enforcement of the new customs duties, he had the support of the Pennsylvania assembly and most of the Philadelphia merchants; but approval of the Stamp Act lost him support at home and his post as Pennsylvania's colonial agent in London. Only his famous appearance before the Commons the next year to urge repeal of the act restored him to favor back home. But he remained in an ambiguous position vis-à-vis the British ministries. Franklin, the Whartons, the Gratzes, and some other wealthy Philadelphians were interested in gaining a royal charter for the proposed new colony west of Pittsburgh. Since this would embrace land claimed by both Virginia and New York, the Pennsylvanians needed ministerial support in London. By the most careful lobbying Franklin had won approval from the Lords of Trade and Plantations when events in Boston blasted the project. In addition Franklin, restored to his post as colonial agent for Pennsylvania in 1766, and also serving in this capacity for Georgia, New Jersey, and Massachusetts by 1770, was continuing his campaign against the proprietorship. It is not hard to imagine that these two long-range projects must have seemed more important to him than passing disputes over tariff duties. But Franklin's indiscreet revelation of some anti-colonial letters of former Massachusetts governor Hutchinson—and the Boston Tea Party—led to his fall from favor with the ministry. Only then did he become an advocate of resistance.

Franklin's difficult balancing acts in London, however, reflected those of his Quaker constituents at home. Only resistance to the Stamp Act united the Quakers and other merchants. At this juncture the upper class had scarcely thought of armed resistance. But even in peaceful Philadelphia mobs prevented the sale of stamps. At the call of Massachusetts, representatives from nine colonies, including Pennsylvania, met in New York and recommended an "association" of merchants pledged not to deal in British goods. Since 1765 was a year of recession partly as a result of the end of the recent war and partly of the Stamp Act itself, this first nonimportation agreement was quite effective. Meanwhile, after a cessation of all business needing stamped paper, lawyers and other users began operating in defiance of the act. Less than six months of nonimportation and nonenforcement led to repeal of the tax by Parliament in 1766.

By the time the Townshend tariff duties of 1767 on tea, glass, lead, paper, and paint brought a new movement for nonimportation, the situation in Pennsylvania had significantly changed. Only about a thousand citizens prosperous enough to meet the voting requirement of owning taxable property worth £50 or more held a majority in the legislature. The more radical Whigs, unable to gain control of the legislature, with the support of workers and artisans were resorting to mass meetings. The rhetoric of even moderate Whig leaders such as lawyer John Dickinson was moving toward resistance to all taxation by Parliament, and to Quakers this portended great danger of violence. Accordingly, the Pennsylvania and New Jersey Annual Meeting of Friends condemned nonimportation as a means of resistance.

From this time onward Philadelphia and the rest of Pennsylvania were deeply divided, not so much over the iniquity of parliamentary taxation, as over what should be done about it. Those in favor of organized resistance were called Whigs; those opposed were classed as conservatives or loyalists depending on their degree of support for the imperial status quo. The divisions were more in accord with religious and liberal-conservative feelings than class lines based on wealth and position. Leading Presbyterian and Anglican merchants might support strong measures, but really devout Quakers could not. Since more than half of the score of largest taxpayers were Quakers, this gave an appearance of upper-class Toryism, but the rich Jewish merchants, such as the Simons, the Frankses, and the Gratzes, supported resistance, as did Anglican Robert Morris, freethinker Benjamin Franklin, and, ultimately, many Quakers including John Dickinson and the later Continental General Thomas Mifflin. Some of the completely unco-operative Quakers were ultimately sent by the Revolutionary assembly to a farm colony in Virginia.

In 1770 all the obnoxious British taxes except that on tea were repealed by Parliament, and prosperous trade relations between mother country and colonies reached new heights. The Parliamentary act that was to precipitate trouble came almost accidentally in 1773. The British East India Company was in financial difficulties and was not able to pay taxes on the transshipment of its tea through British ports and still compete with that smuggled from the Dutch East Indies. To undercut the Dutch price, the new act repealed taxes collected in Britain and allowed the company to ship tea directly to the colonies and sell it there through its own agents, subject only to the colonial tariff. In the colonies advanced Whigs regarded this as an effort to seduce them into accepting the principle of an import duty. Everywhere there was resistance to landing East India Company tea. The Philadelphia pattern of armed demonstrators pursuading the ship's captain to take his tea elsewhere was the one most widely used, but in Boston when the loyalist administrative authorities decided to protect a landing, the demonstrators, disguised as Indians, boarded the vessel and threw the tea overboard. The Boston Tea Party led to punitive laws by Parliament, closing the port and altering the form of local government; they soon became known as the Intolerable Acts.

The Massachusetts Committee of Correspondence now called for a congress of representatives from all the colonies to decide upon retaliatory action against Britain. Ironically, while the Pennsylvania provincial assembly was undecided as to whether any measures should be adopted, Philadelphia, because of its central location between the northern and southern colonies, became the natural meeting place for those planning reprisal. More to calm things down than to take action, the Pennsylvania assembly elected representatives to the First Continental Congress, which met in Carpenter's Hall near Chestnut Street on September 5, 1774. Of the seven Pennsylvania delegates, three, at least, could be classed as conservatives, but they could not prevail against the excitement of the times that favored activists.

The adoption of a plan for "associators" to enforce nonimportation, a victory for the radical position, came as an unpleasant surprise to many Philadelphia merchants. In fact, the radical advocates of nonimportation had a false idea of the importance of the northeastern American trade to the British. In the great panorama of Empire trade major shifts were continually taking place in scales equal to the effects of American efforts at restriction, and London businessmen often failed even to keep in touch with events in America.

The outbreak of war in Massachusetts in the spring of 1775 threw Pennsylvania politics into eighteen months of confusion, during which a Committee of Public Safety wrested power from the conservative assembly, and a new state constitution, breaking the political grip of Philadelphia merchants by giving equal representation to all counties and abolishing property requirements for voting, was adopted by nonlegal popular acclaim. Yet, even though the radical minority, encouraged by Philadelphian Thomas Paine, was getting its way in local and state affairs, Thomas Willing and Robert Morris remained members of the provincial delegation to the Second Continental Congress that met in the Pennsylvania statehouse May 10, 1775.

These partners showed the emotional strains that impinged upon other leading merchants. Both had attended school in England, many of their British correspondents were old friends, and they wished to prolong relationships as long as possible. As Congressional delegates the two business associates had instructions as confused as were their own feelings: from the old assembly a command to vote against independence, and from a newly elected provincial assembly a command to vote for it. When the inevitable ballot was taken on July 2, 1776, Willing and Charles Humphreys dissented, Franklin, James Wilson, and John Morton voted affirmatively, while Morris and John Dickinson, probably on opposite sides, were absent. Both Willing and Morris felt the move for independence was premature; but in August when the official Declaration had been prepared by the printer, Morris saw no use in further abstention and signed the document, as did a new Pennsylvania delegate, George Ross.

By this time the war with England had been in progress for more than a year, and Delaware Bay was patrolled near its mouth by British cruisers. Large vessels fit for the stormy transatlantic crossing were too easy to see, and too slow to evade the Royal Navy; but the sloops and fast schooners used in the southern coastal and West Indies trades could wait in small inlets for the coming of darkness and usually evade the blockaders. Even if a ship was caught, the loss was moderate. The scarcity of sugar in Philadelphia and of wheat in the West Indies made profits in the trade rise so high that Robert Morris said one safe exchange of cargoes on the round trip to the French or Dutch West Indies would make up for "two or three or four losses." If European goods could be disposed of to the Willing and Morris agents in Charleston or some North Carolina port, both profits and safety were still greater. Morris called this trip "the golden voyage." [2]

This new direction of trade from the food-, lumber-, tobacco-, and indigo-producing colonies to the West Indies in exchange for European goods from the neutral islands brought a

2. Clarence L. Ver Steeg, *Robert Morris: Revolutionary Financier* (Philadelphia: University of Pennsylvania Press, 1954), p. 16.

realignment of mercantile interest and revenues in Philadelphia. The most prestigious of the older Philadelphia merchants, such as the Whartons, had specialized in the no-longer-existent British trade, while West Indies voyages, requiring less time and capital, had been in the hands of younger men, such as Willing and Morris (the latter only forty in 1774). Consequently some of the most important members of the big partnerships turned to other activities during the war and never revived their mercantile connections.

Thomas Wharton, Jr., exemplifies the transition from merchant to Revolutionary political leader. The Whig faction rewarded him for his efforts to sway the Pennsylvania assembly toward opposition to Britain by making him a member of the provincial Committee of Safety in 1775. This and its successor, the Council of Safety, were in reality the executive bodies that formed the government by summoning an extralegal constitutional convention. After some months of delay a constitution for the commonwealth was adopted, and Wharton was elected president of the supreme executive council in March of 1777, equivalent to being the first governor of the commonwealth. Other men turned to organizing manufactures to take the place of British goods. At least two efforts were made to stimulate cloth production by establishing "factories," where hand spinners and weavers were hired by the day. One of these, financed by an importer Samuel Wetherill, who had specialized in painter's colors, survived the war, but ultimately he returned to making or importing paints, dyes, and chemicals.

To understand the situation of the Philadelphia businessmen from 1777 to 1780, it is necessary to turn to the overall aspects of the war. In early 1777 the struggle seemed to be going well for the British, and General Howe in New York decided to occupy Philadelphia. This was accomplished after a defeat of Washington's army at Brandywine Creek in September. Extreme Whigs, as well as the Continental Congress hastily left the city, but the majority of the business population remained and prospered from British military expenditures.

During the ensuing winter a depleted Continental Army remained at Valley Forge to prevent the British from invading the surrounding countryside. New life was given to the Continental cause in October 1777, however, by the surrender at Saratoga, New York, of a major British army led by General Burgoyne.

Meanwhile the French were watching the British situation to determine the possibility of winning a world war by supporting the colonists. The defeat of Burgoyne was perhaps the decisive factor that led the French, early in 1778, to give way to the pleas of the American emmissary, Benjamin Franklin, and enter the war. The combination of defeat in upper New York and the threat of French fleets and armies made it appear wise for the British to concentrate their northern forces in New York City. Accordingly they left Philadelphia in the spring of 1778. By 1780, however, the French prosecution of the war had been proven as ineffective over the vast distances of the American seaboard as had the British, and the latter now turned the struggle into a war for trade by attacking the Dutch island of St. Eustatius in the West Indies in 1781. At about the same time, France led Spain into the war against Britain, but Spain did not become an official ally of the United States.

The departure of the British from Philadelphia led a more confident commonwealth government to confiscate the land of admitted Tories in 1778 and the Penn estates in the following year. No compensation was offered by the state to the Tories, but the Penns were promised a settlement of £130,000. In 1780 the state led the nation in abolishing slavery for all children born in the commonwealth and thereafter for anyone over twenty-eight years old.

Throughout the war, Robert Morris was the most important agent in the supply of the Continental Army and became America's greatest merchant. In the Continental Congress from 1775 to 1778, he ran the Secret Committee of Commerce, which had to secure necessary foreign supplies for the army. Civilian goods for Willing and Morris could use up extra space on the same vessels, and the able William Bingham, who handled government exchanges at Martinique, became the local representative of the two Philadelphia partners.

Bingham, who was later to play a leading role in Pennsylvania business and politics, was, in 1776, a twenty-four-year-old English aristocrat who had left the British consular service in the West Indies to join the Americans. When French entry into the war (1778) destroyed the neutral status of their West Indies islands and trade began to decline, Bingham led Morris to enter into an agreement with a Captain Ord for the capture of British vessels. To bring such private seizures within recognized international law, Congress issued letters of "marque and reprisal" to the ship captains. Ord had spectacular success, bringing in thirteen British vessels for condemnation in French, Dutch, or American ports. While Morris was one of the major venturers in this privateering, it was taken up by merchants in all the trading colonies to make up for the commerce interrupted by the war. Essentially they were importing British goods by seizure, and the costs were the shares given the crew and an occasional vessel lost to the enemy or the elements.

Entrance into the war by France, Holland, and Spain made both trade and privateering a risky and complicated business. Except for the challenge by French Admiral de Grasse in late 1781 and early 1782, the British fleets were supreme, but the ocean was full of privateers of all the warring nations as well as naval frigates and cruisers. Often ships captured by one side and recaptured by the other before reaching port. And while war within the United States virtually ended with the surrender of Cornwallis at Yorktown in the fall of 1781, the war at sea went on during most of 1782. On the whole, American privateers made profits that are estimated to have reached a peak in 1780, but success was a matter of luck. Insurance premiums of 40 percent on a voyage to the West Indies indicates about a one-in-three chance of capture.

Stephen Girard, one of the great businessmen in the history of the United States, appears to have lost money in privateering. Eldest son of a middle-class Frenchman who was a burgess and captain of the Port of Bordeaux, young Girard suffered one unlucky trade venture after another; he was driven first to the West Indies, then to New York, and finally, for lack of drinking water on a storm-torn ship, to Philadelphia. When he set up there in June of 1776 as a merchant interested in both French trade and privateering, he was only twenty-six years old.

Though a net debtor, he survived and ultimately prospered in spite of losses at sea, partly because he had brothers and French friends who were traders. But until the end of the war his success was moderate. In the 1780s he was still discharging debts a decade old to Bordeaux merchants, showing by contrast that the great profits of Bingham and Morris included an element of luck. Also the American correspondents used by Bingham and Morris were probably more reliable than were any available to a young foreigner.

Girard married a Philadelphian in 1777, moved to a country place in Jersey during the British occupation of the city, lost a ship with the British departure, and became an American citizen in 1779. Although he was only fifteen years younger than Morris, the heights of their careers fall in widely different periods. Morris was at the peak of his personal fame and fortune in the 1780s, Girard not until the War of 1812. These two most successful Pennsylvania businessmen of the period before 1830 also differed in looks and personality. Morris, a very normal-looking, well-fed Englishman, was out-going and optimistic. Girard, a strong-nosed, small but striking Frenchman, was serious, very reserved, and, perhaps because of his early bad luck, cautious. Morris was eventually ruined by overly bold speculation and died practically bankrupt. Girard, a private banker from 1811 on, left $7 million—the greatest fortune then ever known in the United States—chiefly to the City of Philadelphia for educational purposes.

But these events belong to a later time. As 1777 ended, Girard was still an obscure merchant on North Water Street, and Morris was the principal financial emigré from the British-occupied city of Philadelphia. At this time the term of the Willing and Morris partnership contract came to an end, and perhaps for strategic reasons it was not immediately renewed. Willing stayed in Philadelphia during the British occupation and made some settlements of their British accounts. In 1778 Morris left Congress to devote more time to his personal affairs, which were in turn sources of strength for the young nation.

Morris now became America's leading merchant, a one-man conglomerate apportioning his very considerable financial resources among nine major partnerships. He was involved in the tobacco trade in the Chesapeake Bay and Virginia ports, in the buying of condemned loyalist properties, in supplying the French and American armies, and in many trading ventures.

In a broad view specie dispersed in America for food by large French and British armies, imported goods sold by privateers or inland smugglers, and rising quantities of unsecured paper currency issued by both Congress and the states created a strange, rapidly changing economy, to which Morris and some others, generally young men, adjusted successfully. Paying for goods in specie and first-class bills of exchange, the British and French armies flooded the country with sound but highly varied money. Girard wrote that in Philadelphia in 1777, beside Spanish pieces of eight (dollars) there were in common use "English and French guineas, the Joe or Johannes and its half, quarter, eighth and sixteenth, the Spanish pistole, French pistole, the Moidore, the Doubloon, the English and French crowns, the shilling and sixpence, the current value of all of which were [sic] settled by state tariffs." [3] Meanwhile Congress was issuing paper currency in dollars, with no attempt at any backing from revenues until the first requisition for funds was tendered to the states at the end of 1777.

Requisitions from Congress for money had no force behind them, and in any period of rapid inflation taxes are inevitably inadequate. Reassessments of property don't keep pace with the deteriorating value of money, so that even if taxes are fully paid, they turn out to be insufficient to meet expenses. But in addition, lacking any systematic national assessment of taxable property, people in each state thought that they were being overtaxed for the common good and refused to pay fully. Since tax collectors were generally elected officials, it was rare for them to prosecute a delinquent. In other words, the breakdown in revenue was local as well as national. That runaway inflation, in spite of wildly unbalanced "budgets," continued issues of paper, and large increases in specie, did not take place before

---

3. John B. McMaster, *The Life and Times of Stephen Girard: Mariner and Merchant,* 2 vols. (Philadelphia: Lippincott, 1918), 1:13.

the winter of 1779–1780 is an indication, not only of the hoarding of coins, but of the initial scarcity of circulating money in the colonies.

The mounting variety of different monies gave rise to full-time note brokers in the major centers. One of these, Haym Salomon, had a dramatic career. This thirty-five-year-old Polish Jew, who came to New York from Europe at about the beginning of hostilities, possessed great gifts for languages and for understanding the intricacies of international monetary exchange. Arrested in New York as a patriot spy by the British in the autumn of 1776, he was bound over to a Prussian commander to assist the mercenaries with their language and purchasing problems. These duties did not prevent him from doing some private trading and marrying Rachel Franks. His secret work for the Revolutionary cause among the Hessian troops became evident to the British, and to avoid imprisonment or worse, he fled to Philadelphia, where apparently he soon became a broker officially purchasing and handling exchange for the French. By 1781 he had formed a partnership with Jacob Mier on Front Street and was advertising a wide variety of bills of exchange. He also had become the chief exchange broker for both the governments of the Confederation and of France. During these later years he was the main supplier of foreign exchange to Superintendent of Finance of the Confederation Robert Morris, who relied on his advice. Salomon also won the friendship of many members of Congress by assisting them in their personal financial problems at no charge in commissions or interest. Although he must have amassed a modest fortune by the time of his early death in 1784, he had unquestionably risked his money and his life in the Revolutionary cause.

Since official measures to alleviate the monetary crises of 1780 and 1781 lead one directly into the postwar financial world of Philadelphia, and by 1781 military action in the area had ended, it is better to postpone such history in favor of a brief look at the business of the Pennsylvania backcountry during the period of actual hostilities.

The rather surprising price stability from 1775 to mid-1777 was due, in part, to a surplus of Pennsylvania farm products caused by the decline in exports. Later, however, buying of supplies for the British army in New Jersey and Philadelphia and requisitioning of supplies for the Continental Army (generally paid for in paper currency adjusted for depreciation) restored demand for farm products in the southeastern counties. In 1779 and 1780 southern Jersey and Pennsylvania had good crops and, together with Philadelphia, enjoyed prosperity in spite of runaway paper currency inflation. In an economy used to barter, farmers, manufacturers, and merchants readily adjusted debits and credits on their books without recourse to settling accounts with buckets full of depreciated Continental and state currency, or trouble with laws governing the value of such paper.

To the few thousand nearly self-sufficient settlers beyond the Susquehanna River the war must have seemed remote. The only military actions were against the Indians in the very thinly populated northern and western regions, where there were occasional repercussions from earlier troubles. Sending grain and lumber to Baltimore was the normal activity of the more thickly populated area around Chambersburg and York, and the British interfered less with trade in the Chesapeake than in the lower Delaware.

The great new source of demand in the backcountry was munitions for the Continental Army. Pennsylvania ordinarily exported nearly half of all colonial iron, consequently there was no shortage of metal. The main problem was lack of skilled gunsmiths, ironmasters, and steel mills capable of producing rifles and muskets. A small armory that could produce all types of munitions had operated (in spite of British laws) at Carlisle from 1761 on, but it could not suddenly be expanded to equip an army of thousands of men. The same could be said of the small number of gunsmiths and five (illegal) steel works in the rest of the southeast. Consequently, while Pennsylvania could do more than any other single colony to equip troops, it could not suddenly produce supplies for an army of 5,000 to 10,000 men, and much reliance had to be placed on the roundabout process of importing muskets from Europe.

Wartime demand and the British occupation of Philadelphia increased the importance of Lancaster and other interior cities, paving the way for the rapid westward movement of population in the years after the war. Deserting Hessian soldiers became new skilled workers and re-enforced the Germanic character of middle Pennsylvania. But all in all, it was a seacoast war with only occasional expeditions into the backcountry, which was much too vast for the size of the British armies. Furthermore, while Britain had ultimate power on the sea, naval force in the days of sail was a slow and hit-or-miss affair. The French fleet of Count de Grasse was ultimately defeated at the Battle of the Saints in the West Indies, but not before, in the absence of the main British squadron, it had forced the surrender of General Cornwallis at Yorktown—a position taken by the unlucky British commander because it could be supported from the sea.

As in the history of later industrial development, Pennsylvania's part in the Revolution was geographic and economic. Philadelphia as the largest and most central city of the colonies, occupied by the British for only some nine months, was the natural political meeting place. Some of the city's merchants, particularly Robert Morris, provided economic and financial leadership, and its agricultural backcountry was a principal source of supplies for the armies; but seen as a whole, the Revolution in Pennsylvania was a group effort, not one by brilliant individuals.

3

Basis of the Business
Revolution

*T*HE vigor generated by the businessmen and other leaders of a new nation aided by fortuitous world events brought two generations of truly revolutionary progress in the economic life of the northeastern seaports. But the prosperity was preceded by a period of uncertainty over foreign trade and troubles in meeting the financial obligations incurred for the Revolution.

When the overissue of Continental currency made it essentially worthless by the spring of 1780, Morris, as a private citizen, had helped to arrange supply of the armies by contract, chiefly with merchants who were paid partly in specie supplied by relatively small loans from France, but mostly in Continental promises to pay. Thus mercantile credit, largely from the seaport cities, made it possible to maintain armies in the field after the near breakdown of Continental finance. In July 1781 Morris took official control of the process by accepting the new office of Superintendent of Finance for the Confederation.

Morris now strove to find a means of supplying Congress with money for paying off the army, providing an adequate peacetime revenue, and developing an acceptable plan for funding, in long-term interest-bearing bonds, the various forms of Continental indebtedness. For immediate assistance he proposed creating a Bank of North America. This institution had been preceded by a Bank of Pennsylvania, chartered in 1780 to facilitate dealings with the army contractors, but not designed to do a true commercial business or remain as a permanent financial intermediary. It was liquidated completely in 1784. The new BNA, chartered by Congress in December 1781 and by the State of Pennsylvania in April 1782, was expected to be a lasting financial intermediary for the central government, and served as such until the First Bank of the United States was chartered ten years later. Without special government affiliations the BNA continued as a leading metropolitan bank until its merger with another Philadelphia bank in 1929.

Except for European central banks closely affiliated with their governments, the new Bank of North America was the first chartered commercial bank in the world. It opened for business in January 1782 with Morris's former partner Thomas Willing as its careful and knowledgeable president. He modestly set up shop by renting an office belonging to his partner Tench Francis on Chestnut Street below Third. As he described it two years later:

> When the bank was first opened here, the business . . . was a pathless wilderness . . . little known to this side of the Atlantic. No book then spoke of the interior arrangements or rules observed in Europe. Accident alone threw in our way even the form of an English bank bill. All was to us a mystery, but something was necessary to be done to assist the public measures. In this situation, we adopted the only safe method to avoid confusion. Educated as merchants, we resolved to pursue the road we were best acquainted with. We established our books on a simple mercantile plan, and this mode . . . has carried us through, so far, without a material loss or even mistake of any consequence.[1]

The bank had an initial capital of $400,000, which was supposed to be subscribed in specie by the stockholders, but actually the specie came largely from a French loan to Congress deposited by the superintendent of finance. The bank succeeded

---

1. N. S. B. Grass, *The Massachusetts First National Bank of Boston, 1784–1934* (Cambridge: Harvard University Press, 1937), p. 43.

from the start. Its notes were accepted, deposits built up, and by 1784 it had imitators in both Boston and New York.

Not all Pennsylvanians were pleased with the BNA. Business all over the Western world was generally depressed by the ending of military demand—especially in America because of uncertainties regarding the resumption of former types of trade. Philadelphia, for example, had been a major exporter of food and lumber to the British West Indies, and this trade was now closed to a nation outside the empire. As a substitute Girard and others moved into the Far Eastern trade and also tried to promote more exchange of goods with France and other Continental nations.

But profits from new trades, while ultimately large, were slow in coming. A voyage to the Far East and return by way of Europe, for example, might take over a year. In general, Americans, even in financing their own exports, could not compete with the English and Scotch in terms of credit. Morris, for example, found that the Scotch merchants previously involved could hold on to most of the American tobacco trade between the Chesapeake and France by offering better terms.

Depressed markets in 1784 and 1785 generated a demand for an issue of state currency based on mortgages, as in the colonial period. Led by the legislative representatives from farming areas, the state government, in 1785, issued £100,000 of unsupported paper that was used to cover mounting deficits and £50,000 to be secured by mortgages on land. This action eased the money situation for farmers and other businessmen in the counties normally having an adverse balance of payments with Philadelphia—areas that seldom saw BNA notes. This currency also illustrates how slowly the new dollar replaced the long-familiar pound in state and personal accounting. The issue was not made legal tender, and did not appear to have an inflationary effect. Since Philadelphia no longer had a strong influence in the state assembly, the BNA charter was revoked by the same session that issued the notes, and for two years it operated as a private bank. Articles by Thomas Paine and other Philadelphians finally convinced the newly elected legislators that banks were useful, and the charter was restored in 1787. In 1793 the anti-BNA faction, aided by financier Albert Gallatin of Fayette County, secured a charter for a rival Bank of Pennsylvania with its office in Philadelphia. By 1810 two more banks had been chartered by the commonwealth.

With Washington's help, the army was demobilized, but the veterans received most of their pay in paper certificates. Aside from the BNA, Morris was unable to implement his financial program. Funding the war debts required some reliable congressional revenue, and the most expedient way to obtain revenue would be to transfer the collection of customs duties to Continental control. Morris and Alexander Hamilton, of New York, calculated that a five-percent levy on all imports would be sufficient. In predicting the necessary unanimous consent of the thirteen states neither man reckoned with the unwillingness of New York and Rhode Island to give up their chief source of state revenue. If tariff duties were turned over to Congress, the farmers in both states would have to make up for the loss by a sharp increase in property taxes. Consequently, the Confederation never secured a reliable source of income; Morris was unable to fund the debts and, feeling that his usefulness was at an end, he resigned in the spring of 1784.

The pressure of creditors, merchants, and conservatives of all types, finally brought action in 1786 and 1787. With the grudging approval of, but not any help from the Continental Congress, a group of leaders meeting at Annapolis, Maryland, called for the election of delegates to a federal convention to convene in Philadelphia. While Congress was still meeting in New York, the new Convention assembled at Independence Hall on Chestnut Street in May of 1787. Although in the western counties of Pennsylvania there was resistance to this nationalist movement, the easterners and those favoring stronger central government won control of the state assembly, which elected an eight-man delegation to represent the state at the Convention. These representatives, including Benjamin Franklin, Robert Morris, Gouverneur Morris of the aristocratic New York family but now a Pennsylvanian, and the distinguished Philadelphia lawyer James Wilson, played important parts in drawing up the new United States Constitution. Still under the control of the eastern conservatives, now called Federalists, Pennsylvania in December 1787 followed Delaware as the second state to ratify the new frame of government.

In many respects the Constitution created an effective government for the promotion of economic developments at the then current level of technology. Needed improvements in local areas could be promoted by the "sovereign" states, while the Constitution guaranteed interstate commerce free of tariff duties and mutual recognition between the states of the sanctity of contracts. The new government gave the northern seaports the competitive incentive of essentially autonomous city states combined with the advantages that came from operating in a protected, peaceful market.

The early policies of the new government were also stimulating to business, particularly in Philadelphia. Alexander Hamilton, as Secretary of the Treasury, won congressional approval for funding both the state and Continental debts incurred for the Revolution at par (the face value of the certificates). Since Philadelphia businessmen had long held a great many of the securities, and hastily bought more when they heard of Hamilton's plans, many millions of dollars accrued to the local community. The next year Hamilton secured from Congress, now meeting in Independence Hall, a charter for the Bank of the United States, with a capital of $10 million, to be located in Philadelphia. The capital was raised by selling shares at $400 each, to which the government subscribed for one-fifth. The bank would be the depository for government money, do a general commercial business, and establish branches anywhere in the United States. The ever reliable and most experienced Thomas Willing became its president.

The basis had now been laid to release the pent-up entrepreneurial energies of the post-Revolution generation of American businessmen, and the initial stimulant, as it had been in England, was a great upswing in foreign trade. While in England the eighteenth-century increase in overseas commerce gradually set in motion the business changes leading to industrialization, in the United States the reaction was swifter, stimulated by funding of government debts, rapid urban growth, and more financial aid from the competing states. Nevertheless, the American trade upswing that began at the end of the 1780s seems basic to the speed of the development.

The nearly continuous wars in Europe from 1793 on, brought the British, as controllers of the sea, and the Americans, as the chief neutrals, as close together in trade relations as they had been during the colonial period. From 1789, when United States foreign trade reached the pre-Revolution level, to the close of 1807 British trade was the backbone of the maritime prosperity. Being neutral, ships flying the stars and stripes could go to ports that were forbidden to British vessels, and could make the routine voyages between England and the United States with less danger of attack from enemy privateers, and hence at lower insurance rates. Never again in times of peace were American ships to carry cargoes as valuable in relation to the national income, or representing as big a percentage of all international import and export trade as they carried in the years up to 1807.

From then until 1815 international troubles were practically continuous. In order to weaken the British, whose prosperity depended on trade, Napoleon Bonaparte, controlling the western European states by 1807, concluded an agreement with the Russians to close all ports to British imports. President Jefferson, harassed by British violations of neutral rights, decided that if the United States joined in the European "Continental System" of exclusion, the government in London would negotiate a satisfactory agreement. Accordingly, under heavy administrative pressure, Congress passed the Embargo Act, closing American ports to all foreign trade.

During 1808 the embargo hurt the United States more than it did Britain, because British interests were helped by an upswing in West Indies and Latin American trade. Recognizing the futility of the embargo, the administration ended it in 1809, but the great trade boom was not resumed. Troubles with both France and Britain interfered with shipping until early in 1812, when war with Britain led to a fairly effective blockade of the Atlantic ports.

In Philadelphia the upswing in commerce after 1789 took new directions. Denied the highly profitable British West Indies trade by imperial regulations from 1775 until the Jay Treaty of 1794, and only on an unsatisfactory basis thereafter, the big merchants such as Girard, Morris, Bingham, Franks and Simon, and Willing and Francis looked for new opportunities. Although they had lost their nearest and most reliable customers, the British West Indies, freedom from imperial restrictions opened up the rest of the world. Now Philadelphians could trade with China, India, or the nations on the Mediterranean and Baltic seas, and directly—rather than via Britain—with the nations of Western Europe. Girard kept most of his ships in the Far Eastern and French trade—when the latter was reasonably safe from British attack—but most of the others formed important new British or Dutch connections for Russian and other European trade.

In London before the Revolution John and Francis Baring had been merchants of modest size interested in American trade and close to Hope and Company in Amsterdam, then the world's chief financial center. On occasion the Barings had done business with Willing and Morris, and at the close of the war, Morris wrote suggesting that they take an active interest in Philadelphia trade. By this time, under the inspired guidance of Francis Baring, who was most adept at handling government transactions in foreign exchange, their house had grown greatly in wealth. They were now among the most important London merchant bankers, and they determined to make a specialty of American relations, with Morris, Bingham, Willing, and Robert Gilmore of Baltimore as their chief correspondents. The Barings' reliable connections in the Baltic area and on the Continent were of great assistance to the Philadelphians entering on new trades.

By 1795 the suggestion by Bingham that the Barings invest in Maine lands led to the sending of Alexander, second oldest son of Francis (now Sir Francis, Bart.) to America. Although Alexander landed in Boston, Bingham had him met by a special representative who escorted him to Philadelphia. Alexander bought a million acres of Maine land owned jointly by Bingham and General Henry Knox for $400,000. But he also saw many other chances for profit for the firm, and, enjoying life in the highest social circle of the capital, he stayed on. In 1798 he married Bingham's daughter Anna Louise. This and the marriage of another Bingham daughter, Maria Matilda, to Alexander's brother Henry in 1802 symbolize the commitment of Baring Brothers & Co. to a century of interest in American affairs.

From 1791 on, the Barings were the European agents for the Bank of the United States, and were generally employed to facilitate American government payments or collections abroad. After 1803 the Barings also represented Stephen Girard. In the course of these many early relationships, the Barings were responsible for transferring millions of dollars in investment capital from Britain to the United States; in 1809, for example, foreigners owned 18,000 of the 25,000 shares in the Bank of the United States.

With Dutch, French, and Spanish ships largely eliminated from their normal trades because of Napoleon, and the risks of capture even of neutral vessels forever changing, merchants worried continually and profited enormously from inflation. South American trades, ordinarily monopolized by Spain, as well as the Far Eastern trades of France and Portugal were opened to adventurous American merchants. Scarce commodities brought double and treble their usual value.

While all of this wartime activity was also creating a larger demand for American goods and bringing in handsome fortunes to successful merchants, it was actually benefiting New York more than Philadelphia, because of New York's more accessible port for all but the West Indies trade. Consequently, while both cities prospered, the great upswing in trade was the first of the factors that led New York, by 1810, to surpass Philadelphia in size.

In 1790 Philadelphia had entered a new world of high demand and unusual affluence that produced a revolution in the ways of doing business only slightly foreshadowed by the banking developments of the 1780s. The "revolutionary" developments were exciting achievements by local entrepreneurs in new enterprises. The changes came in greater efficiency resulting from size and specialization. The numerous functions of a mercantile office like that of Willing and Morris were split up into separate firms for banking, insurance, wholesaling, brokerage, real estate mortgaging, and ultimately into concerns dealing only in certain commodities. The incentives for such separations had been present from the 1770s, but it took the combination of the forces of demand in the 1790s to bring them about. The improvements all had one thing in common, they saved time, and time was the greatest element of cost. In the rapid expansion of business, the immediate need was for working capital—for the money that was tied up while goods were in production, stored as inventory, or in long, slow transport. Therefore a new method or facility that saved time at any of these stages was of major importance in cutting capital costs. Speeding up production led to division of labor so that workers might become specialists at one task. It also prepared merchants to consider the use of more or better machines, particularly for transportation.

Most of the new advances, however, were of a purely business or managerial type. For example, merchants began to use joint stock associations and corporate charters. A chartered corporation had its powers and methods of operation prescribed in a legislative act, whereas a joint stock organization was a strictly private group that drew up its own rules. Both types benefited from freely salable shares of stock. In Britain joint stock associations had been severely restricted because of early-eighteenth-century scandals, and there had been grave doubts about their legality in the colonies. Whether or not a colonial governor might grant a charter for private purposes had also been questionable.

In both Britain and Europe a charter for a business enterprise had to be passed on by the national legislature or some central council. All of these bodies, including Parliament, were influenced by a traditional aristocratic contempt for and suspicion of businessmen and their motives. Even when a company had some public purpose, such as improvement of transportation, a British Parliamentary charter took influence, money, and time. Furthermore, the government took no positive interest in the success or failure of such enterprises.

In contrast, the American state legislatures, composed of a small number of farmers and businessmen anxious to develop their home areas, were willing to charter almost any corporation with whatever rights and privileges seemed necessary to promote local enterprise. Hence American entrepreneurs were able to draw upon the accumulated savings of farm and city by marketing shares of stock in ventures ranging from sound banks to risky manufacturing firms. Important internal-improvement companies, as well as banks, could also sell stock to the states.

The corporate form led to better bookkeeping, or what may be called the beginning of accounting. The old-style merchant made no distinction between personal and business accounts. Partnerships, of course, had to make this separation, but they generally neglected to draw up periodic statements of profit and loss. Only the more advanced businessmen used double entry, or read the texts on bookkeeping that began to appear in Philadelphia and other cities in the last half of the 1790s. Corporations, however, with stockholders who wanted to know how the company was financially, used double entry, periodic statements of profit or loss, and necessarily treated the firm as a separate entity. These three principles—double entry, periodicity, and the separate entity of the firm—were the basis of nineteenth-century advances in accounting.

Two events of 1792, the formation of the Insurance Company of North America (INA) and the charter of the Philadelphia and Lancaster Turnpike Company illustrate the use of the stock company in aid of business development. While from 1752 on, fire insurance had been available from the Contributorship, there was no company ready to write marine casualty insurance at a scheduled premium. Shipowners had to waste time shopping around among merchant underwriters or applying to the agents of London companies. It was said to be difficult to place locally a large policy such as one over $25,000.

The INA, with a $600,000 capital, promoted by highly respected Philadelphia merchants, was organized in the main room of Independence Hall in November of 1792. This use of a room in the national capitol for public meetings testifies to the smallness of the combined government operations of the nation, the state, and the city who shared the use of the buildings. A state charter for the company was delayed by the opposition of private underwriters, by the great yellow-fever epidemic of 1793, and ultimately by the opposition of another group seeking a charter. Finally, in the spring of 1794, both INA and the rival Insurance Company of the State of Pennsylvania, promoted by Thomas Willing, were chartered.

Lack of a charter had not prevented INA, as a joint stock company, from doing an increasing business from its two-room office on South Front Street. Meanwhile, as the war in Europe made American vessels safer than British, there was plenty of business for both companies. During the trade boom, marine casualty was the most profitable, although risky, underwriting of both companies; the companies also insured against fire and issued an occasional life policy, for which there was little demand.

A turnpike was a more novel and complicated venture than insurance. The latter had been a logical spin-off from the business done by the old-style mercantile office, employing the same men doing the same tasks but on a larger scale and in a specialized way. A turnpike involved construction with crushed stone, a type of road not hitherto used in America, and for distances that would require the use of several local contractors. When the road was finished, tollgates would have to be arranged in some way that would force payment by users of the road and honesty in accounting by the collectors. Finally, since the road required extensive repairs each spring, maintenance would be an annual problem.

An interest in better transportation was not new in Pennsylvania. The state assembly after the Revolution had voted to construct turnpikes and bridges at state expense. But modern Telford or Macadam-type turnpikes of crushed stone were expensive, and the state failed to act. Finally a private association, comprised mainly of Philadelphians and called the Society for the Promotion and Improvement of Roads and Inland Navigation, put pressure on the legislators to charter private corporations to connect Philadelphia with Lancaster, and ultimately with the Susquehanna River. Leading members of the society, Bingham, Morris, and Willing, formed the Philadelphia and Lancaster Turnpike Company, which readily secured a state charter. Bingham, by accepting the presidency, gave an aura of security and reliability to the enterprise.

It apparently did not seriously bother Bingham or his associates that he was a financier rather than a man with technical knowledge of construction. Americans, like Europeans, believed that any man of good intelligence should be able to run a business. While Bingham had the usual troubles with contractors' estimates and inspection, problems involved in construction at a distance from the head office, he devoted much attention to the project and probably did as well as could be expected. Construction was completed in 1794 at a cost of $465,000, or about $7,000 per mile. In spite of nine tollgates, the cost of moving goods from Lancaster to Philadelphia was cut by about two-thirds.

Bingham and his directors initiated the idea of division superintendents, later to be used by the railroads, and demanded daily reports from these officers. One feels sure that such a flow of information was never secured, but rising competition from other routes rather than managerial trouble appears to have been the problem of all turnpikes. The more roads that were built either by governments or by mixed or private companies, the easier it was to avoid tollgates. Unlike a railroad or canal that required a special means of conveyance, a road could be departed from or entered on at any point. Hence, while the Lancaster road earned reasonable dividends for some years, by 1800 it was only paying about 2 percent on its stock.

The relatively poor financial showing of the Lancaster Pike deterred private investment in similar ventures, but the popular demand for improved roads was so great that with state subscriptions to stock and granting of outright subsidies, turnpikes continued to be built. As was to be the case with railroads, local investors may often have bought stock more to show support of community enterprise than with any expectation of adequate returns. Even if unprofitable to owners, these roads were of great economic value to their communities.

Another specialized form of business that made its American debut in Philadelphia was organized stock trading. In 1791 ten merchants who wanted to trade in securities met at the Merchants' Coffee House, organized a Board of Brokers, and elected Matthew McConnell president. Half a dozen years later a more formal association adopted rules and an entrance fee. New Yorkers followed with an initial group in 1792 and at daily meetings in both cities lively trading went on in securities such as shares in the Bank of the United States.

That brokers still met at an old coffeehouse calls attention to the compact business area of the capital city, which particularly in the first half of the 1790s kept much of its old look. The Bank of the United States, for example, occupied Carpenter's Hall, while the Library Company moved into its new building nearby on Fourth Street. Not until 1797 was the stately First Bank building on Third Street finished. Meanwhile, as we have seen, the federal government was sharing the buildings on each side of Independence Hall with both the state and local authorities.

The central area of the nation's political and business capital of the 1790s was still easy to traverse in a few minutes' walk. Mercantile offices extending along Front Street a little beyond High Street (Market) formed the northeastern end, and Fifth and Walnut streets, the southwestern end. While there were some businesses further away than this, they were regarded as beyond the main commercial area. Such compactness, possible for a city of less than 75,000 people, meant that business could be conducted reasonably expeditiously without telephone, telegraph, or a clearing house for the four banks.

The backcountry, which had made Philadelphia the greatest colonial city, continued to increase rapidly in population and to stretch further and further westward, but with diminishing benefit to the metropolis. Along the southern border of the state, beyond the Susquehanna and across the watershed of the Allegheny Mountains, the expansion at this period was of little trade value to Philadelphia. Towns such as York and Chambersburg were much nearer Baltimore than Philadelphia, and even Harrisburg was about twenty miles closer to Chesapeake Bay than to the Delaware. Philadelphia connections were injured by improved navigation of the Susquehanna to the Maryland line in the 1790s, but were aided by the extension in 1794 of the Lancaster Pike to Columbia on the river below Harrisburg. Meanwhile, of course, Baltimore was promoting Maryland turnpikes and canals up the Susquehanna and Potomac rivers. Where goods were sent depended on their bulk and type of market. Grain from these border counties went largely to Baltimore. Local manufacturers might seek the bigger and more reliable market of Philadelphia. For purchases, the Philadelphia market was superior, so that money collected for grain at Baltimore might buy imported fabrics at the northern city. The cost of moderately valuable manufactured goods was not increased much by the slightly longer wagon trip west.

Somerset and Cambria counties, lying mainly west of the headwaters of the Juniata River—which was navigable only for small boats eastward to the Susquehanna—had to be largely self-sufficient. In 1783 the roughly seventy-five miles of poor road from these counties to Pittsburgh and the more than two hundred miles to Philadelphia nearly isolated the farmers in their valleys and uplands. For exchange of goods with the outside world they relied largely on driving farm animals over the mountains or marketing home-distilled whiskey, which could be taken in fair quantities on packhorses to the nearest trade centers or to inns along the main roads.

It was this reliance on whiskey as a medium of trade that led these settlers into a brief rebellion against an excise tax levied by Congress on their product. The resistance speedily collapsed before an exaggerated show of military force by the federal authorities in 1794, but the "Whisky Rebellion" illustrated the difference of economic interests in the state between east and west.

As Pittsburgh and its region grew from the 1780s on, the merchants at the Forks of the Ohio were ultimately able to market farm and iron products down the river, but could not bring bulky goods upstream. As the early trade system matured, Pittsburgh farm products and timber could go down the Ohio and Mississippi rivers and be sold at New Orleans, but the proceeds were best spent in Philadelphia, from whence the special products not available in the Pittsburgh area could be shipped west at a cost in the early 1800s of about six dollars per hundred pounds. From 1785 on, the state improved the road from Chambersburg and Bedford over the mountains to Pittsburgh and kept it passable for wagons and mail. By 1800 it was dotted with tolerable inns for the business traveler and heated barns for the wagoners, and in 1804 a stagecoach line operated between Philadelphia and Pittsburgh. In fact, one is rather surprised at the ease and relative comfort with which Philadelphia merchant Joshua Gilpin and his family traveled by private carriage from Philadelphia to Pittsburgh in 1809, to inspect his western land holdings.

That Gilpin would undertake the long journey of over two weeks each way attests the importance of the west in the thinking of wealthy Philadelphia merchants. Real estate had, of course, been the chief type of investment since William Penn's original plan of compelling the purchase of backcountry acreage along with town lots. The late-eighteenth-century development of the region beyond the mountains came partly as the result of two Indian treaties, both at Fort Stanwix (New York) in 1768 and 1785, which finally freed the northern and western parts of the state from the continual threat of attacks by the Iroquois. The other necessary prelude to speculation and settlement was divestiture of the proprietory land of the Penns by the state in 1779.

While holding the price of unoccupied land in general at a high level of over fifty cents an acre, the state set up a number of special arrangements for gifts of land. In the northwest corner almost to Lake Erie, ''Donation'' lands in amounts of from 200 to 2,000 acres, according to military rank, were reserved as bonuses for those who had served in the troops of the Pennsylvania Line during the American Revolution. South of this reservation along the western border, including the Pittsburgh area, ''Depreciation'' lands could be bought with certificates used to pay soldiers during the war. In addition 52,000 acres were given to western educational academies and several western state reservations were surveyed for town sites, on one of which Pittsburgh was built.

This all sounds quite enlightened and systematic, but it wasn't. The element lacking was any adequate administration of the land office. As was to be the case practically everywhere, soldiers sold their rights to investors at very low figures, and wealthy men came to own vast acreages. Adding to the confusion was a Homestead Act of 1792, by which actual settlers on western land could buy it for from two to six cents per acre. Between 1792 and 1794, five million acres were taken up by people claiming to be settlers but who actually were acting for a few land companies. In 1799 a considerable part of this land, such as that acquired by Robert Morris for the Holland Land Company, was attached by the state, and the action lasted so long and was so costly that no one profited. None of the other hastily organized land companies appear to have made a profit, but men like Gilpin who carefully selected smaller acreages through reliable agents and who supervised both rental to tenants and sale, appear to have done better.

Loss was not unusual in the history of "wild land" speculation in the United States. Administration, policing, surveying, taxes, and waiting for settlers often drained the resources of companies that were usually started with insufficient capital and with stockholders interested in too many other ventures. The period after 1793 was a particularly unfavorable time. The land operators counted on the continual flow of European immigrants that had built up the colonies, but the Revolutionary and Napoleonic wars in Europe stopped extensive emigration until after 1815. As a result even astute businessmen such as Robert Morris found themselves overloaded with unsalable land. The great dream of Europeans flocking to the cheap farms of the new nation faded for a generation. Morris was finally ruined because settlers were not attracted to buy his large holdings in the District of Columbia before the government's move to Washington. In accordance with the law of the period, not altered in Pennsylvania until 1833, Morris had to go to debtors' prison in Philadelphia, where looking at the great financier in the prison yard became a tourist attraction.

Relatively few who invested in distant lands made much during their lifetime. Tench Coxe, a Philadelphia merchant and prolific writer on economic subjects, as well as Assistant Secretary of the Treasury under Alexander Hamilton, bought thousands of acres in the unpopulated northeastern area of the state, and while he was always pressed to meet the payments due, his descendants became owners of some of the state's richest anthracite coal lands.

Perhaps the distinguishing feature between the men who overextended themselves in land speculation and those who stayed within safe limits was the degree of their optimism. While Morris, always hopeful, went too far, the more cautious Willing had little to do with such schemes. Bingham, as we have seen, enlisted the support of Baring Brothers in his moderate venture in Maine lands. Girard invested only moderately in Kentucky and western Pennsylvania and kept most of his money in trade, banking stocks, and property in or close to Philadelphia.

Buying cleared farmland and leasing it to newcomers who lacked capital was an operation quite different from investing in wild land. Many of the purchasers of cleared farms were prosperous nearby farmers, merchants, or mill owners. As English, Scotch-Irish, or Welsh farmers depleted the soil by continuing antiquated methods, production fell in the area around Philadelphia and gave landlords a strong business interest in improving agriculture. In 1785 a group organized the Philadelphia Society for Promoting Agriculture, which tried to assemble information from all over the nation. In 1809 large landholders organized the Pennsylvania Society for Improving the Breed of Cattle, and throughout this period agriculture was the subject of many papers read at the American Philosophical Society. These societies persuaded the state legislature in 1820 to authorize and assist county agricultural societies.

But real progress on the farm was slow, practices were traditional, and "book farming" was often ridiculed. Farmers of German ancestry preserved fertility better than the others because they had come from areas of Europe where limestone or animal fertilizer and fallow seasons were in use, and they—the sectarians, particularly—planned permanent residence. Consequently a German owner or tenant would repair some of the damage done by farmers who traditionally exhausted the soil and then moved on. A general pattern in the southeastern area was that as small farmers moved west, larger operators substituted dairying and meat raising for the growing urban markets in place of the previous soil-exhausting staple crops; but such a shift obviously required some capital investment.

Land either wild or improved was far from the only form of investment for the merchants prospering from foreign trade. All of the older industrial and processing activities of the state were expanding and requiring more capital. More iron furnaces and forges were started between 1780 and 1800 than in all the previous period, and presumably much of the money came from Philadelphia. But there was no major change in iron technology or in the size of operations. In spite of bituminous coal lying next to the veins of iron ore in the western part of the state, smelting was still done by charcoal. While nails and supporting structures for ships and bridges were made in Pennsylvania, good tools and implements of iron and steel were largely imported.

More efficient waterwheels for mills kept the use of steam power before 1808 commercially negligible. John Fitch ran steamboats on the Delaware from Philadelphia to Burlington, New Jersey, in 1788 and 1790, but the homemade low-pressure engine and awkward paddles supplied too little power for carrying freight and moved the boat too slowly to attract sufficient passengers. Fitch was unable to raise capital for further development. In 1802 there were two high-pressure steam engines in Philadelphia; one was crushing plaster of Paris, and Oliver Evans was experimenting with the other. Two years later he ran a new higher-pressure steam engine on wheels around the city's streets, but again no capitalist saw a profitable use for steam in transportation. This had to wait for the *Clermont*. With a substantial investment by Chancellor Robert Livingston of New York, Philadelphian Robert Fulton designed the boat with a large engine; the *Clermont* navigated the Hudson to Albany in 1807. Two years later a steamboat built by John Stevens of Hoboken, New Jersey, ran from Burlington to Philadelphia.

A Pennsylvania Society for the Encouragement of Manufacturers had been founded by a group of Philadelphia merchants in 1787, but a fire destroyed the spinning factory it had erected in

1790. One of its members, John Nicholson, a close associate of Robert Morris, tried to establish an incredibly ambitious manufacturing complex of button, glass, spinning, and iron factories at what was later to be Manayunk. But he was far too overextended to operate his factories successfully. Aside from the mismanagement shown in the Nicholson venture, the application of machinery to textile manufacture faced unusual difficulties in the Philadelphia area. Household manufacture of thread and of low to medium grades of cloth had become well organized by the end of the colonial period. While thread spun in efficiently run mills could theoretically undersell the homemade product, in weaving, the machine processes of around 1800, even for coarse cloth, had little if any advantage over handwork. Consequently, in the period from 1790 to 1815, although Philadelphia and the surrounding towns were the major textile producers, there was less effort at mechanization than there was in New England.

Because of many opportunities for skilled or semiskilled workers, Philadelphia was a relatively high wage city. Since such labor organization as appeared was limited to the highly skilled handicrafts, the city was a leader in union activity. In 1792 the local shoe employees formed the Federal Society of Journeyman Cordwainers, which lasted only until a strike was lost. Organizations of journeyman printers and tailors had much the same history. In 1800 a Pennsylvania court found strike activity to be a common-law conspiracy in restraint of trade, a doctrine that was only gradually altered in any of the states. The most important industry in the city, building construction, was little affected before the 1820s by either unions or changing technology. Always America's chief need for capital investment, construction prospered greatly as shops, offices, and houses grew more numerous and spacious, yet perhaps because many workers contracted independently for their services, no permanent labor organizations appeared in the building crafts during the early period. Carpenter's Hall was an early creation of masters not workers.

When in December 1807 President Jefferson checked trade by his embargo on exports in American ships to foreign ports, the state and the nation were prepared in business institutions and new technology for a rapid advance. Banks, brokerage houses, specialized wholesalers, and insurance companies were prepared to handle an increasing volume of business. Hard-surfaced turnpikes connected the major eastern cities. Oliver Evans was selling improved steam engines. Local processing in food and wood products was in some cases leading the world in new mechanisms. And Philadelphia was one of the world's important centers of shipbuilding. But the seven years of interrupted trade and war with Britain that followed prevented the rate of growth anticipated by the properly optimistic businessmen of 1807.

4

The National Financial Center

$\mathcal{P}$ENNSYLVANIA and the nation went through two distinct economic phases before 1850: first, the essential development of business institutions capable of organizing and financing national industry and transportation; second, the rapid growth of canals, railroads, and industry, particularly coal and iron using machinery powered by steam and increasingly efficient. The first phase matured by the mid-1820s, the second, by the mid-1850s. In the second period, Pennsylvania gained a national supremacy in heavy industry that lasted until the end of the century. Before the close of the two periods, Philadelphia's position as the nation's financial center had finally ended with the demise of the Second Bank of the United States in 1836; but by then the migration of financial influence northward had been going on for over a decade, and New York was already more important as a general money market.

Philadelphia's initial financial supremacy was built on its size, central location, and economic support of the Revolution. The supremacy continued because as the national capital for the decade of the 1790s it became the site of the First Bank of the United States. The city's growth was also supported by the local prosperity in the area of eastern Pennsylvania, northern Delaware, and western New Jersey. These early advantages over its urban rivals were prolonged by the embargo of 1808 and the War of 1812, which struck harder blows at the economic well-

66

being of New York and Boston, cities that depended much more on ocean trade than did the southern metropolis with its self-sufficient economy.

Regardless of other factors, the location of the First Bank of the United States in Philadelphia in 1791 made the city the center of banking influence. Since the bank was much the largest in America, actually one of the largest banks in the world, and its operation was closely tied to the federal government, its financial structure is of interest. Capital was set at $10 million with the government owning one-fifth or 5,000 shares at $400 each. The hard-pressed United States Treasury had to borrow $2 million from the bank to subscribe for its shares. The government had ten years to repay its loan, but other stockholders had two years to pay for their shares, with one-fourth in specie. The twenty-five directors all had to be United States citizens; six were to be replaced annually and were ineligible for re-election. The bank could establish branches anywhere in the United States, and its notes, redeemable in specie, were to be accepted for all federal payments. Business organization of the bank, of course, preceded stones and mortar, so for nearly six years it operated from Carpenter's Hall, before moving into its permanent quarters. The new building, Philadelphia's finest in Corinthian classic, was located on the west side of Third Street between Chestnut and Walnut, a block often called "the cradle of American finance."

Thomas Willing's resignation as chief executive of the Bank of North America and his acceptance of the presidency of the Bank of the United States (BUS) symbolizes the dual nature of the bank. On the one hand, it was to be a new kind of bank with as yet undefined obligations to produce some type of central system in the United States; on the other hand, it was a major Philadelphia financial institution doing business alongside the other two banks. That it performed both functions well is due in no small part to the even-handed and objective administration of "Old Square Toes."

The local banking situation in the ports of New York and Philadelphia necessarily influenced the policies of the Bank of the United States. With the chartering in Philadelphia of the

Bank of Pennsylvania in 1793, the state began a policy of investing in bank stock, one-third of the capital in this case. Of all the state investments in corporations, only those in banks earned reliable dividends, and protecting these brought the state actively into problems of bank competition.

In 1803, when the Bank of Philadelphia sought a charter, the state owned $1 million worth of stock in the Bank of Pennsylvania, from which it received $80,000 annually in dividends, the largest item in state income. After a sharp legislative battle, the sought-for charter was granted in 1804 only on the basis of the new bank paying the state $135,000 as a bonus, and allowing a state subscription to its stock. The Farmers and Mechanics Bank, chartered in 1809, also had the state as a stockholder and was bound to have as directors a majority of "farmers, mechanics, and manufacturers actually employed in their respective professions." [1] This clause, which because of large establishments in iron, leather, furniture, flour milling, and shipbuilding, scarcely kept out big capitalists, shows the popular conception of manufacturing as skilled and small-scale.

But in spite of the growth of local banking and the location of the Bank of the United States, Philadelphia never equalled London or Paris in its influence as a national financial center. In 1791 there were, in effect, four banking systems, each operating around one of the major northern ports. Not until 1794 did the two most important become regularly interconnected on a day-to-day commercial level by Philadelphia's Bank of North America arranging with the Bank of New York for a standing $40,000 credit to be used for purposes of exchange. Consequently, there was no demand that the Bank of the United States take on responsibilities as a central clearing house, and Willing wisely dealt with the state banks as completely autonomous entities. Yet, because of treasury transactions in taxes the Bank of the United States was necessarily a creditor of each local bank, 89 of them by 1811. It did not attempt, however, to use the interest rate charged on these obligations as a lever for

1. Bray Hammond, *Banks and Politics in America: From the Revolution to the Civil War* (Princeton: Princeton University Press, 1957), p. 165.

regulating the money market, and since it was forbidden by its charter from owning federal bonds, it could not expand the currency in circulation through buying such bonds in the securities market.

Albert Gallatin, the United States Treasurer from 1801 to 1814, joined Willing in moderate efforts to control the specie reserves of banks, either by leaving the federal deposits of customs and other tax collections in the local banks, or by moving them to the BUS in Philadelphia. Another means used for affecting the quantity of money available was through the timing of new federal loans or the repayment of earlier issues. Willing and his board also tried to keep the notes of state banks, which continually passed through the BUS, on a reasonably sound basis by occasionally demanding redemption of considerable quantities in specie. On a few occasions the Bank of the United States helped sound banks that were temporarily in trouble. Perhaps most important of all, it moved federal deposits from points of collection to where the money was needed. From 1801 until 1807, when illness forced Willing to resign, he had the cooperation of a most remarkable Pennsylvanian as Secretary of the Treasury.

Albert Gallatin seems like a romantic hero straight from historical fiction. A Swiss nobleman of distinguished ancestry, he was brought up and educated to the age of nineteen in Geneva, one of the chief European centers of learning. Here he was surrounded by the most advanced European thinking in philosophy, science, and practical affairs. The twentieth-century mystique of the Swiss in banking had been foreshadowed in the eighteenth century when their financial practices together with those of the Scotch were commonly regarded as the world's models.

To avoid a career in government bureaucracy, distasteful to a disciple of Rousseau, Gallatin came to Massachusetts in 1780 "for his own freedom, not hers." [2] An orphan, Gallatin was to receive a modest patrimony when he reached the age of 25, in 1786. By mortgaging this in advance to M. Sevary, representing a French mercantile house, the young immigrant became the ad-

---

2. David S. Muzzey, "Albert Gallatin," *Dictionary of American Biography,* 4:103.

ministrator, and ultimately half owner of 120,000 acres in southwestern Pennsylvania. There, a few miles up the Monongahela from the Virginia line, Gallatin built a country place, Friendship Hill. But like so many young upper-class believers in the virtues of nature, he was soon unhappy in his isolated surroundings and as a way back to the world of urban sophistication took to the politics from which he had fled.

For a decade Gallatin served as the local intellectual leader in western Pennsylvania affairs. He attended conventions, served in the legislature and on most of its committees, and drafted resolutions and bills. As a reward Pennsylvania sent him to the United States Senate in 1793, but the Federalists were able to unseat this learned backcountry follower of the liberal Jeffersonian Republican party on the basis of too short a term of citizenship. Gallatin's home district countered by electing him to Congress, where he served until 1801. By this time he had formed a committee on finance (the later Ways and Means Committee) and so harassed the Federalist Secretaries of the Treasury that he became the undisputed Jeffersonian financial leader.

It was fortunate for Willing and the Bank of the United States that so understanding a financier became Secretary of the Treasury. Jefferson and, to a lesser extent, Madison were strong opponents of the bank, while Gallatin, recognizing its essential role, continually shielded it from political interference. In the course of doing so he alienated many members of Congress, but it is hard to see how anyone could have done better than this broadminded, even-tempered Swiss aristocrat. He tried to use Treasury policy to stabilize banking and the money markets, and kept in close touch with Willing. Since the period includes a war against the Barbary Pirates of North Africa, the Louisiana Purchase, the embargo, and other interruptions of normal revenue and trade, Gallatin's and Willing's tasks were far from easy. In addition the Bank of the United States as the chief dealer in foreign exchange tried to keep money at reasonable rates available to businessmen for making payments to other areas of the United States or to foreign nations. Bray Hammond, a later secretary of the Federal Reserve Board, speaks of "the excellent record of the Bank." [3] In fact, the United States has probably never since enjoyed so good a banking system. Later attempts at system have suffered because of the unwillingness of state banks to support a sufficient degree of national control; that was not the case in the two periods of the Banks of the United States. Victory for the nationalists in the first period was a result of action taken before local opposition was organized; in the second period, as we shall see, it came only from an extreme postwar financial emergency.

While the lasting opposition to central banking has been from weak state banks and local businessmen desiring easy credit, in 1811 when the charter of the Bank of the United States was to expire, its recharter was also opposed by many farmers and planters afraid of all urban money power. Typical of this opposition was a memorial from eighty citizens of Pittsburgh, a city which, in reality, could and did gain substantially from having the financial center of the nation within the state. It declared that the bank "held in bondage thousands of our citizens who dared not act according to their consciences for fear of offending British stockholders or Federal Directors." [4] The gross misunderstanding behind their prejudice is shown by the fact that only American citizens could vote stock and that Stephen Girard of Philadelphia was the largest shareholder, but not a federal director.

Perhaps it is remarkable that in the congressional roll calls on recharter the bank lost by only one vote in the House, and by the tie-breaking vote of Dewitt Clinton, as Vice-President, in the Senate. The Clinton vote mirrored New York state banking opinion against the institution that so aided Pennsylvania. Among the Manhattan banks only the old Bank of New York joined the Philadelphia banks in petitioning Congress for recharter.

By selling 2,220 shares to Baring Brothers in 1802, the Treasury had disposed of the last BUS stock originally subscribed to by the United States government. About 1809 Stephen Girard

3. Hammond, *Banks,* p. 208.
4. Hammond, *Banks,* p. 213.

decided that because of international uncertainties he should bring home about a million dollars owing to him from Europeans. He took back over half of the amount in goods, but also bought about a thousand shares of Bank of the United States stock from his London correspondents, the Barings. As the recharter decision approached, he increased his holdings sufficiently to have a powerful influence in the ultimate settlement of the bank's affairs.

When an attempt to charter the Bank of the United States in Pennsylvania was defeated by the same type of localism that defeated it in Congress, Girard bought the bank building on Third Street and opened the private Bank of Stephen Girard with a capital of about a million dollars. In the gradual liquidation of the affairs of the former Bank of the United States, creditors received their full due and shareholders the par value of their stock. But meanwhile, with the same cashier and about the same staff, Girard was conducting private banking on a scale that rivaled the big chartered banks.

Girard's decision to proceed on a private basis came only after an effort to gain a charter had been defeated at Lancaster (then the capital) by the state banks, anxious to restrain such strong competition. From beginning to end Girard, although a Jeffersonian Republican, was never popular with state politicians, probably because of the jealousy of the Philadelphia banks, which promptly joined together in refusing to accept his bank notes for deposit. He was much cheered, however, by a letter from London in August of 1812. The famous Alexander Baring wrote:

> I have long been of the opinion that such an establishment was wanted in America and could not fail of success. . . . People cannot transact business confidentially with 24 directors . . . and are besides exposed to the jealousy and observation of their neighbors. A private Banker will be found so great a convenience that I think it probable [sic] you will have almost all the commercial houses for customers.[5]

5. McMaster, *Life and Times of Stephen Girard,* 2:241.

The end of the Bank of the United States could scarcely have happened at a worse time for the nation. With the War of 1812 only a year away, local banks doubled their note circulation and increased in number, starting an inflation even before the British blockade deprived the government of essential customs revenues and forced it to borrow large sums of money for military expenses. The result was some eight years of financial disorder, particularly marked in western Pennsylvania and the Ohio Valley.

To finance the war, for which no preparation had been made in the way of emergency taxes, Congress authorized a total of $61 million in bonds. The extremely able Gallatin as Secretary of the Treasury tried to offer only the amounts that the market could absorb tolerably well. This meant much financing by short-term treasury notes. In all Gallatin and his successors issued about $45 million in bonds, which brought in some $34 million in specie value. The first major Treasury crisis arose over the attempt to issue $16 million in six-percent bonds in 1813. Initial subscriptions only came to about $4 million, and after further efforts Gallatin turned to three of America's most prominent financiers—John Jacob Astor, Stephen Girard, and David Parish—to form a contracting syndicate. John Jacob Astor was a wealthy merchant of New York and David Parish an American representative of European banking interests. Although they had already subscribed heavily, the three men agreed to take most of the remainder of the bonds at a fair price, and Girard ended up personally holding the largest share. To the Philadelphia bankers this was another menacing example of Girard's financial power, based not only on his own great though unrevealed wealth, but also on his connections throughout the western world.

For four years after opening his bank in 1812 Girard's operations were discriminated against by the local banks, which jointly agreed not to accept his bank notes, and by state laws that threatened the notes' legality. A law of 1810 prohibited note issues by partnerships or other unchartered associations, but did not specify single private citizens. While the state authorities would probably not have dared to try to apply the law against Girard because his able lawyers, such as Alexander J. Dallas and the Ingersolls, would no doubt have proved it unconstitutional, in fact, the law was not generally enforced against any group. The important Farmers Bank of Lancaster, for example, defied it with impunity. Early in 1814 the state passed an act offering 41 bank charters to applicants from those areas of the state needing better banking facilities and again prohibiting all issue of notes by unincorporated banks. A result of the Pennsylvania law and similar actions in other states was an increase in the total number of chartered banks from 89 in 1811 to 260 in 1816, with a sevenfold or eightfold increase in notes in circulation. In course of time Girard was duly cited as in violation of the law, but the governor, under pressure from Girard's attorneys, quietly removed his name from the list of violators. By 1816 the Philadelphia banks, needing Girard's help, agreed to accept his bank notes, and he became a fully participating member of the local banking community.

Girard's victory over banks and legislators was due not only to his having outstanding lawyers and friends such as Secretaries of the Treasury Gallatin and Dallas, but also to the near breakdown of American finance between 1814 and 1816. The burning of Washington by the British in 1814, and fear that Baltimore might be next, brought a general suspension of specie payments by bankers south of New England. The latter would now, of course, accept southern bank notes only at discounts. Girard shipped his specie to Reading for safekeeping, and apparently continued business much as usual. Meanwhile, Gallatin had resigned as Secretary of the Treasury to join the peace commissioners in Ghent, and his three successors between 1814 and 1816, including Dallas, were unable to float long-term loans. Astor and Parish were willing to try to place considerable sums in Europe, but Girard, who probably had the most money in liquid resources, would not again join them. With the failure of arrangements for such contracting, the treasury lived from hand to mouth by issuing and reissuing short-term notes. Often there was not enough money for administrative salaries.

To many merchants in the middle-state seaports as well as in the south and west, the solution for the spreading chaos seemed clearly to be a new national bank. Probably stimulated by Astor, fifty New Yorkers petitioned for a bank early in 1814, but the measure failed in Congress. A new bill introduced at the beginning of the following year passed, only to be vetoed by President Madison as inadequate in its provisions. The final bank charter, passed in the spring of 1816, was signed by Madison in April. During these two years Astor and Girard had supported a continuous lobby for a bank, although their efforts were probably opposed by most of the banks in their respective cities. These two merchant-financiers, as well as United States senators Henry Clay (of Kentucky) and John C. Calhoun (of South Carolina), were generally recognized as the most active sponsors of the bank. It is interesting that although a majority of the Pennsylvania members in the House and Senate voted against the bill, there was no serious legislative conflict over the bank's location in Philadelphia.

The Second Bank of the United States, this new and greatest addition proportionally ever made to the financial power of Philadelphia, had an authorized capital of $35 million with one-fifth, as in the earlier bank, to be subscribed by the federal government. Of a twenty-five-man board of directors the President of the United States could appoint five, and the private stockholders could elect the rest, with no single person being allowed to vote over thirty shares. The board, in turn, elected the president. Stock subscriptions were opened at Girard's bank, but the shares, limited to a maximum dividend of six percent, failed to attract the necessary buyers. With the closing date at hand and $3 million in stock unsubscribed, Girard astonished the financial world by saying that he personally would take the rest. This famous action is more interesting as an example of the growing maturity of the east coast money market than of great assumption of risk by Girard. If he had any difficulty in distributing the shares to his correspondents, particularly Astor, it was not recorded. Parish, who had returned to Europe, probably placed some stock there, but Philadelphians, with 88,500 shares, compared to New Yorkers' 20,000, were the chief investors.

Astor, Gallatin, or Girard could have had the presidency of

the Second Bank had any of them wanted the office, but Astor's affairs were centered in New York; Gallatin preferred foreign service; and Girard was willing only to become a government director. The unwillingness of the nation's chief financiers to serve as president led to the appointment of Captain William Jones, a Philadelphia merchant lacking experience with large-scale banking, who had served briefly in 1814 as Secretary of the Treasury. (In all, eight Pennsylvanians held this post between 1800 and 1850.)

While New York was rapidly outpacing Philadelphia as a trade center, and hence increasingly jealous of the latter's possession of the central bank, the earliest difficulty was with Baltimore. The charter placed a maximum on any individual's vote but did not prevent a stockholder from distributing his holdings in one-share trusts and then voting each of them separately. By this means a Baltimore group was able to outvote Girard and other conservative bankers and elect a board favorable to continued expansion of credit.

Alarmed by the lax policies of the group in control of the bank, Girard in 1818 refused to continue as a director. A great real estate boom was in progress in the Ohio Valley, and the Chillicothe and Cincinnati branches of the BUS were feeding it with currency available for loans and bank-held mortgages. Hence, in spite of the deflationary effect of the resumption of specie payments in 1817, the land boom continued. Meanwhile, Girard as chairman of a group of the largest stockholders secured a congressional amendment to the charter, which gave control to the owners of a majority of the shares, and in 1819 they replaced Jones as president with the conservative Langdon Cheves of South Carolina.

Cheves abruptly reversed the bank's policy from expansion to contraction. While necessary in the long run to save the bank, the liquidation of loans was more severe than necessary. The branches suffered from the effects of both policies. Overexpansion had had the effect of taking some business away from the local banks; contraction created a panic in the money markets. In Maryland the legislature, strongly opposed to the Bank of the United States, passed a bill to tax the Baltimore branch $15,000 a year. In the case of *McCulloch* v. *Maryland* the federal Supreme Court upheld the constitutionality of the bank and its exemption from state taxation, but the Baltimore troubles were not over.

Not only had the branch overexpanded credit, but the cashier, James McCulloch, and two leading merchants had embezzled some $1.5 million of Bank of the United States funds. Embezzlement was neither a common nor, in Maryland, a statute law crime (it had only been so in Britain since 1799), because the money stolen had been, either by subscription to stock or deposit, voluntarily given into the custody of the thief as an officer of the bank. In fact, much of the business community of Baltimore supported McCulloch and the two merchants, and in spite of a second trial, ordered by the supreme court of Maryland, the trio was acquitted. Since embezzlement was one of the major dangers in branch banking, this case led to the passage of a number of new state criminal laws.

Cheves suffered the fate of financiers forced to recoup the worthwhile remainders of a real estate boom, and particularly of an expansion that had altered the normal flows of federal money. With large revenues coming in from federal land sales in the west and with most of the bank's payments to be made in the east or to Europe, the Bank of the United States had continually to move funds away from the fast-growing Ohio Valley. No matter that the money had come from the east only shortly before; the people of the west wanted it to stay there. Consequently, feeling against the probably overconservative and unimaginative policies of Cheves mounted until, with the help of President Monroe, the board, unable to secure Gallatin, replaced Cheves in 1823 with Nicholas Biddle of Philadelphia.

Destined to be one of the most important and controversial figures of his generation, Biddle's past goes far to explain both his virtues and his defects. The son of a prominent Philadelphia merchant and politician (his father had been vice-president of the state when Franklin was president of Pennsylvania) Biddle had been an adolescent prodigy. By the age of fifteen he had completed college courses at both the University of Pennsylvania and Princeton, and had gone to London to study law. Like many brilliant men he was uncertain as to what he wanted to do. He cared little for the practice of law, enjoyed service abroad as secretary to the ambassador to Britain, James Monroe, edited a Philadelphia literary quarterly the *Port Folio,* played a minor role in state politics, and in 1817 retired to Andalusia on the Delaware above Philadelphia, an estate inherited from his wife's mother. Meanwhile he had written extensively on finance and agreed to serve as a government director of the Bank of the United States in 1821. Biddle's very considerable virtues were energy, self-assurance, versatility, and an understanding of banking at a time when Bray Hammond doubts "if one banker in four clearly understood what he was doing and what made it sound and proper." [6] Biddle was gracious and witty, although necessarily a bit removed from ordinary businessmen. In fact, one of his defects was a failure to sympathize with and respect business habits and practices. "Knowing he dealt with conventions," writes Hammond, Biddle "ventured to deal with them rationally. The consequences were deplorable." [7] Caring little for money, as a financial leader he came unconsciously to like power.[8] Under attack he lacked ruggedness or patience and misjudged the drifts of politics. Yet, in all, he was the world's leading and most successful central banker of the 1820s.

The power and dignity of the bank under his management was symbolized by the massive Doric building designed by William Strickland, built on Chestnut east of Fifth, and occupied in 1824. From there the growing financial power of the bank was a part of an exceptionally good period in the history of American banking. During these years Biddle increasingly made the bank the chief facility for interregional and international payments. As the cotton trade grew enormously after 1825, it was largely financed by drafts from the branch in New Orleans on branches in the northeastern ports or the head office. It was an ominous but inevitable sign of the future that by 1830 the drafts on New York City for Mississippi Valley cotton ship-

---

6. Hammond, *Banks,* p. 275.
7. Hammond, *Banks,* p. 295.
8. See letter from his wife on "Ambition" in Nicholas B. Wainwright, *Andalusia* (Philadelphia: Historical Society of Pennsylvania, 1976), p. 21.

ments were averaging a level of $4 million a year, almost equal to the total for the three rival ports. While the BUS in Philadelphia managed the interregional money flows, the city was losing the cotton export trade. As more large-scale national business was done in Bank of the United States drafts, payable in the bank's own notes, these notes were constituting a true national currency.

While the Bank of the United States also tried to help sound banks that were in distress, as became a central bank, it could not legally increase the money in circulation by buying government bonds with bank notes. From 1823 to 1836 there was never a severe test of the bank as a lender of last resort. As its business in exchange exceeded that from commercial loans, the latter were left increasingly to state and private bankers. But in spite of this partial withdrawal from competition, the bank's exchange operations reduced the profits of state banks and note brokers, whose rates were forced down.

The real menace to a central bank in Philadelphia, however, was not from the interior money changers, but from Brown Brothers; Prime, Ward, and King; and other powerful Wall Street banks or brokerage houses. Continuously irked by such matters as seeing the largest customs collections in the nation removed from their local money market by the United States Treasury and transferred for deposit to Philadelphia, some bankers and brokers of lower Manhattan used every political means either to end the bank or to transfer it to New York.

The issue of recharter raised in 1831, five years in advance, became so complex politically on a national rather than a Pennsylvania stage, that its history cannot be attempted here. In relation to the inevitable realities of national growth, Biddle's political errors diminish in importance. It is symbolic of the financial drift that when Gallatin returned from Europe in 1827, during the period of the greatest influence of Chestnut Street, he took a position in New York City rather than in Philadelphia. From 1830 on it was only the bank that kept Philadelphia as the financial center, and it seems inevitable that had the bank been rechartered, at some point an amendment would have been passed to move it to New York as the nation's foreign trade center.

It is true that had Biddle been able to deal with President Andrew Jackson, and been more careful about offending him, a third central bank could have been chartered, and this would have greatly benefited the national economy. Hence there was a Greek tragedy enacted in the temple on Chestnut Street, in the classic form of the hero's ambitions and limitations destroying him and his works. But who can tell what the worldwide depressions from 1837 to 1843 might have done to any financial institution that could be manipulated by essentially hostile leaders in Congress abetted by President Van Buren?

Denied a federal charter by a Jacksonian veto in 1832, Biddle sought and by 1836 had secured a local one under the name of the Bank of the United States of Pennsylvania. But he had to pay too high a price to secure the state charter. To a bonus of nearly $5 million, were added mandatory investments in ongoing state works so that by the time it had to close in 1841 the bank had contributed some $13 million to the state, too much, perhaps, to bear in normal times, certainly too much in time of depression. In addition Biddle from 1836 to his resignation in early 1839 pursued a policy much like that of the largest Wall Street banks of 1929. Too much of the bank's investments were in loans with the nearly unsalable stocks and bonds of canal and railroad companies as collateral, and in claims against cotton inventories being held off the market in hopes of a rise in price. Had the world economy improved in 1839, the bank might have survived, just as the banks of later day might have done had world conditions become better in 1931, but in both cases the reverse happened. Both 1839 and 1931 marked only the beginning of the most severe phase of depression, and in 1840 there was no Reconstruction Finance Corporation to save the big banks.

In fact, the long period of depressed business from 1837 to 1843 may be regarded as the first modern-style depression—one in which industry as well as commerce and agriculture played a major role. Economic historians have traced an American business cycle from the seventeenth century on, but it could readily be associated with economically uncontrollable events such as wars or variations in the size of crops. The panic of 1819 was the first to be distinctly featured by real estate speculation and overexpansion in banking and a few industries. But the decline was relatively brief and recovery was strong by the end of 1822. Recessions between then and 1837 were mild, and few businessmen were prepared for the severity of the decline initiated by President Jackson demanding payment in specie for government land, and the curtailing of credit for cotton purchases by the Bank of England.

From 1837 on, however, all careful businessmen began to think in terms of the business cycle. And correctly so, because Americans, always striving to expand operations too fast, made the peaks of business activities higher and the depths lower than in the older nations. Actually Philadelphians and Bostonians seem to have weathered the storms rather better than their more optimistic neighbors. The Quakerlike frugality and caution that seems to have characterized Philadelphia transactions may have worked against producing brilliant entrepreneurs, such as Rockefeller, Carnegie, or Morgan, but as we shall see in some later instances, local advisors often were correct in restraining entrepreneurs ready to take large-scale risks.

The drama of the Bank of the United States of Pennsylvania ending in the first severe depression tends to obscure several constructive financial developments in which Philadelphia had taken the lead. On December 2, 1816, a month before the opening of the Second Bank, the Philadelphia Savings Fund Society, the first mutual savings bank, announced its readiness for business on two days a week at 22 South Sixth Street. (A five-day-a-week opening came only in 1865). The aim of the society was to encourage saving (capital formation) by workers and servants, money that could be invested in obligations of the United States or the City of Philadelphia. When, in 1818, the society expanded the types of permissible investments, urban mortgages became much the most important. As a mutual, every three years earnings in excess of normal interest payments of a little under five percent and operating costs would be divided among the depositors. While the organization was incorporated in 1819, it preserved "Society" in its title. Within two months a savings bank appeared in Boston, and somewhat later savings banks opened in New York and Baltimore. It is worth noting that for the first two years of operations Boston's Provident Institution for Savings merely deposited its funds at interest in commercial banks.

The banks of this day made no effort through club or retirement plans to encourage systematic saving by the lower-income groups. Consequently, in 1831 two Englishmen who had created successful textile operations in Frankford, not then a part of Philadelphia, joined with other local businessmen in forming a British type of loan fund called the Oxford Provident Building Association. Members who bought five-hundred-dollar shares at five dollars down and three-dollar monthly payments, were entitled to bid for six percent loans up to the value of their shares. The amounts seem small today, but only a tradesman or skilled worker could count on saving three dollars a month, and a good house could be built for less than a thousand dollars. The Oxford's first imitator was the Brooklyn Building and Mutual Fund Loan Association started in 1836.

More important as a source of mortgage money than either of these types of mutual funds was the great growth of insurance corporations in the city in which they had first appeared. The two early fire-insurance companies invested chiefly in short-term mortgages, but the casualty and marine enterprises made personal loans and bought stocks. By 1804 in "insurance row" around Second and Walnut streets there were seven more insurance offices, each underwriting most types of risk. In order to keep better track of incoming ships, in 1807 the companies combined to operate a semaphore type of telegraph from Philadelphia to Reedy Island at the head of Delaware Bay. The British destroyed the equipment of the system in 1813, and quarrels with the patent holder, Jonathan Grout, prevented reconstruction.

Following the war, a group of nine Philadelphia marine-insurance companies was said by a later historian to be much the strongest in the nation. It had the longest experience in estimating maritime risks, and while insurance companies in Boston and New York were more numerous, their profits were lower.

Philadelphia remained the insurance center because of its insurance knowledge rather than for its volume of business.

Investment banking, for which the Philadelphia firm of Jay Cooke and Company was to become famous during the Civil War, was not a distinctly separate branch of finance before 1840. New securities were subscribed to on books opened in the office of the issuing company by individual capitalists, or by banks, insurance companies, or state or local governments. When the whole amount had been taken, the books were closed. Initial subscribers buying directly from the company, such as the commercial banks or individuals like Stephen Girard might then pass the securities on to their customers at a small commission. As we have seen, Girard did this with war bonds and the stock of the Second Bank. When substantial parts of an offering were contracted for, as in these cases, a special price—slightly below that posted—was negotiated. Thus merchants and financial houses were all performing investment banking functions, but not to the extent Jay Cooke did later by forming a syndicate in advance to underwrite or buy up an entire issue.

Aside from a few merchant bankers like Girard (who died in 1831), Thomas A. Biddle, or the Browns who had a Philadelphia branch, brokers such as Francis M. Drexel, and lottery-ticket sellers were among the most active retailers of securities. In 1816 Solomon Allen of Albany moved the headquarters of his lottery and note exchange firm, S. & M. Allen, to Philadelphia. With branches in Albany, Pittsburgh, and other cities the firm did a considerable volume of new security buying and selling. Like the Bank of the United States, the Allens in 1837 held an unusually large amount of newly issued securities that were losing their market value, and the firm was forced into bankruptcy. Enoch W. Clark, originally from Massachusetts, a relative and former partner of Solomon Allen, took over Allen's customers; then Clark and his brother-in-law Edward Dodge began a brokerage and investment-banking firm. In 1839 Jay Cooke came to work with them and was made a partner in 1843. By 1850 the Clark firm, a family organization, had branches in New Orleans; St. Louis; Burlington, Iowa; and New

York City. Like other private bankers, the Clarks and later Cooke with his own firm made money in dealing in bills that transferred money from place to place for a federal treasury that lacked central banking facilities.

During the Civil War Jay Cooke and Company introduced new tactics into the field of investment banking. In 1863 when the government was having trouble selling securities fast enough to meet its mounting obligations, Cooke agreed with the Secretary of the Treasury to market an entire issue of war bonds. His prestige as a Philadelphia private banker enabled him to form a very big underwriting syndicate of bankers of all types across the nation, which could reach most of the people who had money to invest. Helped, of course, by patriotic appeals, his big syndicate made a remarkable sales record and suggested the application of big syndicates to the marketing of new issues of corporate securities. Successfully carrying out such an operation with a Pennsylvania Railroad issue in 1868, Cooke helped to make underwriting by a large syndicate a customary practice. In connection with the mid-nineteenth-century prowess of Pennsylvania in banking, it should be remembered that Anthony J. Drexel of Philadelphia, from 1871 until his death in 1895, was the senior partner of Drexel, Morgan and Company, the nation's most enterprising investment house.

Yet these special elements should not obscure the growing superiority of the New York market. While in the early days of banks, turnpikes, and canals the Philadelphia business in securities exceeded that of New York City, and its stock exchange stood on an equal footing, the accumulation of profits from trade and the rise in the middle 1830s of railroad finance on a scale never thought of before made New York City's investment houses and its stock exchange the national leaders. Another reason for the shift in importance in security trading was the fact that much of the growth in capital investment by Philadelphians was in unincorporated, closely held ventures within Pennsylvania, an early growth that was not matched in the immediate New York City region. Hence, as described in following chapters, Philadelphia capitalists financed much of their own back-country through private partnerships, while New Yorkers increasingly invested their profits from trade in the securities of corporations operating elsewhere. The two money markets thus became, in many ways, incomparable from 1840 on, with national supremacy in public transactions passing to New York, but with perhaps as much real wealth remaining for many years in the hands of Philadelphians, whose transactions never appeared in the public market. While quiet, retiring wealth suited the Philadelphia temperament, the difference seems more the result of economic and geographic circumstances than of compelling regional business cultures.

5

Opening the Inland Empire

URING most of the nineteenth century, unequaled riches in timber, iron, coal, and oil engrossed Pennsylvanians in the economic development of their own state. Although New York City became the great distributing point for imported merchandise, Philadelphia's exports of food and fuel kept it first in outbound tonnage. Meanwhile, iron and other industry developing all over the state stimulated a continuing improvement in transportation. Until 1840 Pennsylvania's transport development exceeded that of any other state. One reason was that its economy came to center around two focal points, Philadelphia and Pittsburgh, each in turn a major port for both local and worldwide commerce. Philadelphia was obviously an ocean port, but Pittsburgh, at the head of the Ohio River, could also ship to the Gulf of Mexico and to the oceans through New Orleans. In the beginning, however, it was the agricultural and mineral resources of eastern Pennsylvania that enticed capital into roads and canals.

We have seen that the slowness of the state to respond to the need for better transportation led Robert Morris and others to form a Society for the Promotion and Improvement of Roads and Inland Navigation in the State of Pennsylvania. Representatives of the society lobbied continuously before the nearby state legislature in Independence Hall, and in 1792 secured a charter, but no money, for the Philadelphia and Lancaster Turnpike

Company. The state government still hoped that private enterprise would speedily solve the transportation problem by such construction.

The new company copied the Telford system of roadbuilding, developed in Britain, using a central strip of crushed stone about twenty feet wide, with larger pieces at the bottom diminishing to coarse gravel at the top, bordered by cleared but unpaved shoulders. The very moderate returns on this busy Philadelphia and Lancaster pike, completed in 1794, however, discouraged investment in roads that could anticipate much less traffic. Aside from companies that built roads from Lancaster to Columbia and Harrisburg, there was little activity during the late nineties. Consequently by 1800 the state was led to step in as an initial subscriber to stock in mixed state and private corporations. Mounting gradually, the state investment in turnpikes reached a par value of $1.8 million in 1825. In a few cases the commonwealth put up most of the actual cash, but, on the average, the face value of the private investment was considerably larger. Such state subscriptions for construction were in addition to the modest annual appropriations for road improvement.

Partly as a result of this government encouragement and partly from optimistic local fund-raising, the major cities of the state as far west as Bedford and north to Sunbury and Williamsport were soon connected by hard-surfaced, gravel turnpikes. The old trail to Pittsburgh, cleared by General John Forbes, during the French and Indian War, was somewhat improved and was made a toll road west of Chambersburg in 1806. A rock-and-gravel surface was completed after the War of 1812. Meanwhile a seventy-five-mile section of the federally constructed National Road from Baltimore to Wheeling, Virginia, on the Ohio River entered the state south of Somerset and, running through Uniontown and Washington, passed some twenty-five miles south of Pittsburgh.

Four- and six-horse red and blue Conestoga wagons with white canvas tops could carry three tons or more on hard-surfaced turnpikes economically enough for trade in dry goods and manufactures, but for moving timber, coal, and iron, canals were needed. The most manageable and productive project appeared on the map to be canalization of the Schuylkill to beyond Reading and from there make a connection with the Susquehanna River. As early as 1762 a survey had been made for a link between the rivers. Thirty years later two companies were chartered to build from the Delaware to the Susquehanna by way of the Schuylkill, but they did not complete any work before the War of 1812. In those days of limited use of iron and coal, and of both abundant timber and iron in the eastern part of the state, the need for canals was less pressing than it would be by the 1820s and the investment needed for turnpikes was both smaller and quicker in producing results.

Responding to continued growth in population and the rapidly increasing demand for iron machinery and coal after 1820, state and private interests in Pennsylvania improved waterways that were three times as long as New York's Erie system and built through much more difficult country. By the 1840s this system was one of the wonders of the western world. In fact, it seems safe to assume that, except for France, no nation in history had ever equaled Pennsylvania's improvement of water transportation within such a brief period, and French construction was easier. A state-financed, toll-free canal circumvented the Conewago Falls on the Susquehanna River in 1797, making Columbia rather than Portsmouth (Middletown) the point for transshipment eastward.

The next canals, completed in the 1820s, were built by private corporations. The first important link was constructed by the Schuylkill Navigation Company, chartered in 1815, which within a decade built a combination of dams with canals and locks around them known as a slack-water system because it could operate when the river was low. These improvements made the Schuylkill usable by canalboats to Port Carbon, 108 miles northwest from Philadelphia. The essential link from Reading on the Schuylkill to Portsmouth just below Harrisburg, completed in 1828, involved difficulties that were not properly assessed by its private promoters. To save time and money in construction, the Union Canal Company adopted a European style 8½-foot-wide lock. This was not the same size as locks of the Schuylkill Company or of locks the state was building westward from the Susquehanna along the Juniata River; both of these systems could take boats 12 feet wide. Factors undoubtedly influencing the decision to use a narrower lock were the difficult terrain and the shortage of water. Perhaps, with the technology of the day, a canal should not have been attempted. Ninety-three locks on its 78-mile length made the cost of any later rectification high, and after the governor vetoed a bill to widen the canal in 1838, nothing was done until too late to be useful. As a result, most Susquehanna Valley freight using this route to Philadelphia had to be transshipped at both ends of the canal, and as the lower Susquehanna became completely canalized by 1841, the heavy or bulky products of the great interior valley, whether bound for Baltimore or Philadelphia, went first to the Chesapeake.

In the long run, however, the inadequate Union Canal was not quite as great a disaster to Philadelphia as might at first appear. The fourteen-mile-long Delaware and Chesapeake Canal, finished in 1832, was just across a narrow stretch of water from the eventual outlet of the Susquehanna Canal. Ironically this key link in the Pennsylvania system, although largely financed by investors from Philadelphia, was outside the state. Delaware Bay was nearer to the end of the Susquehanna Canal than was Baltimore, and going down the Susquehanna to Philadelphia took only a little longer than going to the rival port. When the Susquehanna Canal was opened in 1841, the Philadelphia and Havre de Grace Steam Towboat Company was ready to haul barges to Philadelphia. Yet part of the failure of Philadelphia flour exports to increase substantially between 1820 and 1840 may be laid to the unfortunate Union Canal.

The towboat company calls attention to the great advantages that steamboats brought to the Delaware River cities. It often took days to get upstream by sail from New Castle to Burlington or Bristol. By even a slow steamboat the trip took only a few hours. The river ports of Wilmington, Chester, and Philadelphia became parts of a compact area for the movement of passengers and goods. The same development aided Pittsburgh even more by opening the Allegheny northward and up-stream traffic on the entire Ohio-Mississippi system to the west.

By 1823 the Erie Canal in New York State was nearing completion, and Pennsylvania, particularly in the Philadelphia and Pittsburgh areas, felt that the state must act quickly to preserve its western trade. Committees of the legislature were appointed, investigations made abroad, and for three years the value of a canal as against a railroad was debated. Without ever resolving the debate, a rather panic-stricken legislature passed a bill in 1826 setting up a board of canal commissioners, and one year later, another act authorizing the commissioners to provide for a system of state-financed canals or railroads. The most pressing and important need was for cheaper transport from Harrisburg on the Susquehanna over the mountains to Pittsburgh and the west.

The problem was a frustrating one. With the then current technology, canals using viaducts over the Susquehanna and Allegheny rivers, and a tunnel into central Pittsburgh could certainly be constructed with no more than the usual costs of following winding river valleys such as the Juniata and the Conemaugh. But between the nearest parts of these rivers, only thirty-odd miles from each other, lay a long, impenetrable ridge of the Allegheny Mountains. That thirty miles of rugged terrain should stand in the way of a three-hundred-mile connection seemed unacceptable to the commissioners, and without solving the problem, they began work on the two canals. The man selected to find a method of crossing Allegheny Mountain (which gave its name to the whole range) was a young gentleman from Virginia, Moncure Robinson, who was to make his greatest reputation half a dozen years later by building the Reading Railroad from the Schuylkill County coalfields to Philadelphia with nearly uniform and continuous grades, which meant that not only would equal motive power serve for the entire route, but the same engine could pull heavy loads of anthracite or wheat downgrade and light loads of manufactured goods back up.

The son of a prosperous Richmond merchant, Robinson had

tired of classical education at William and Mary College and had sought to join western survey parties in Virginia. Too young at first, he went as an observer, studying the problems of canals or railroads in mountainous country. This led him to a three-year private inspection of the solutions used in England, Wales, France, and the Low Countries, his boyhood knowledge of French helping him greatly during his two winters at the Sorbonne. When he returned to America in 1828 and went to inspect his father's lands in western Pennsylvania, he was authorized by the canal commissioners to make a survey of a possible portage across Allegheny Mountain. In effect, through the indirect use of the merchant capital that had educated Robinson, the most up-to-date European technology was brought to bear upon the Pennsylvania problem.

After five months of surveying in 1829 Robinson proposed a solution that used devices successful in Europe, but never before tried on such a scale as Allegheny Mountain would require. Five cable railways to take cars up inclined planes would be needed on each side of the summit. Between the lifts, powered by stationary engines, the cars would be pulled by horses or locomotives. The railroad would begin at Hollidaysburg on the Juniata and end over 30 miles west at Johnstown on the Conemaugh. The lift on the eastern side would be 1,400 feet and on the western side, nearly 1,200. The part of the plan that shocked the canal commissioners was a mile-long tunnel through the mountain.

Deciding to get more seasoned professional advice, the commissioners turned to Colonel Stephen Harriman Long, a college-educated member of the Army Topographical Engineers, who in 1829 had published a *Railroad Manual*. Long approved the Robinson survey in general but found a way of reducing the length of the tunnel to 900 feet. He proposed rails of strap iron about ¼ inch thick and 1½ inches wide, attached to the top of wooden beams similar to those used in houses, and the use of steam locomotives on the level sections as soon as possible. On the basis of the Robinson and Long reports and further advice from Major John Wilson, an engineer who had planned the Philadelphia-to-Columbia rail connection, the commissioners let construction contracts for the Allegheny portage in the spring of 1831. The Juniata Canal, already well advanced, involved 108 locks in 178 miles from the Susquehanna to Holidaysburg, while the 102-mile section of canal west from Johnstown, also under construction, reached Pittsburgh through a lengthy tunnel, and both eastern and western canals required viaducts. The entire "Mainline" project, completed in 1834, was financed by issues of state bonds, many of which were sold in England and increased the commonwealth's debt by over $12 million.

Typical of the advanced stage of iron machine building in Pennsylvania were shops at the two ends of the portage railroad that did much of the ironwork, including locomotive repairs and replacements. The whole transit was made more unusual in 1842 when John Dougherty eliminated the absolute need for transshipment by patenting the sectional canalboat, each part of which could be loaded on a flatcar at the portage.

It is worth noting that, while the portage was and has been continually criticized as bordering on the fantastic, it was the product of the thinking of two of the ablest engineers in the United States. The initial cost, while nearly sixty percent higher than the Erie in New York, was not the critical factor in either case. The Mainline, successfully operated for some twenty years after completion, brought important aid to the economic welfare of the state. Its greatest weaknesses were not the inclined planes but the early need for transshipment at either end of the portage and the high maintenance costs of all northern American canals.

The innovations necessary for building and maintaining the state railroad and canal system benefited greatly in later years from the services of a civil engineer from the Royal Polytechnic Institute of Berlin, John Augustus Roebling. Coming from Mühlhausen, Prussia, to Pittsburgh in 1831, he and his brother bought seven thousand acres of land in Butler County for development purposes. Tiring of rather unsuccessful battles with the land, he went to Harrisburg (the capital since 1812) and resumed his career as an engineer for the state. Troubles with hemp cables on the portage railroad gave him the idea of using wire rope; after the usual bureaucratic state resistance, he was allowed to install the rope in 1841. The state system needed many bridges, both to carry canals across rivers and to carry land vehicles over the numerous waterways. As a result Pennsylvania became known as the state of bridges. This practically continuous building gave Roebling a chance to put into practice his theories of bridge construction, which had been his chief interest since college days. At Pittsburgh, in 1846, he built the first true suspension bridge, a long one over the Monongahela. It had four spans of 188 feet each suspended by wire cables 4½ inches in diameter. From this time on, large bridges began to take this form, and Roebling became a world-famous designer and manufacturer of the necessary equipment.

Even before the improvements made by Roebling the state system worked. While tolls were considerably higher than those on the Erie, the Pennsylvania Mainline was the cheapest way of sending most goods from the Philadelphia area to the upper Ohio Valley. The government owned only the facilities and carriage was by private companies. Since the tolls, however, scarcely paid for salaries and maintenance, even the operation of the system was, in effect, state-subsidized. Maintenance was usually the greatest drain on all northern canal revenues. Winter freezes and thaws injured the machinery at the locks, while spring floods inundated the canals along the rivers, destroying banks and towpaths, and filling in the waterway with mud. The Pennsylvania canals traversing mountainous country were particularly prone to flooding.

In order to get legislative appropriations for the Mainline, the state had to build more than a dozen canals or slack-water systems in other parts of the state. The longest of these, the North Branch Division, went from Northumberland at the main Forks of the Susquehanna, north of Harrisburg, on for 169 miles, through Wilkes-Barre to Athens just below the New York border. The West Branch Division went up the other fork of the Susquehanna 73 miles to Farrandville beyond Lock Haven. The Delaware River was also made navigable from Bristol to Easton, over 80 miles upstream from Philadelphia. By 1845 the state-operated canals were administered through eighteen divisions, only five of which were on the Mainline. Since up to the late 1830s all improvements were financed by borrowing when credit was available, they greatly increased the state debt.

While none of these divisions gave the state an adequate return in tolls, the canals of the 1830s greatly aided economic development. In 1834–1835, when the system began to operate, the value of products using some part of the Mainline east and south was $1.8 million; in the years 1836–1840 it was $4.3 million. The same figures for the more valuable shipments of manufactured goods going west or north were $3.2 million and $7 million respectively. The canals not only encouraged private companies to build strategic connecting links, but fostered agriculture, mining, and industry along their banks. The chief private feeders were for transporting coal. Of these, the Lehigh Coal and Navigation Company, between 1827 and 1838, canalized the Lehigh River for 84 miles from Stoddartsville, near Wilkes-Barre on the Susquehanna, to Easton on the Delaware. Other privately constructed canals from Beaver, north of Pittsburgh on the Ohio, reached Erie and Cleveland. Of all the canals, only the Schuylkill Navigation Company appears to have continuously made money from tolls.

In addition to these man-made waterways, the Ohio River flowed north and west from Pittsburgh to the western state line, and the Allegheny from its confluence with the Ohio and Monongahela extended more or less due north, crossing into New York and wandering eastward by Olean, beyond which it returned again to Potter County in Pennsylvania. Early steamboats navigated the Allegheny to Warren less than 20 miles south of the New York border and, by 1845, some slack-water dams opened the Monongahela for keelboats and barges to the southern border. Hence, with the various improvements, the state could be traversed from east to west by water except for 37 miles of portage, and from south to north at the Delaware, the Susquehanna, the Monongahela, and either by the Allegheny to the central New York border or by the Ohio River and connecting canals to Lake Erie. The state constructed system of waterways totaled nearly 800 miles.

In later years the Board of Canal Commissioners pursued a flexible policy of selling where possible to private interests, as

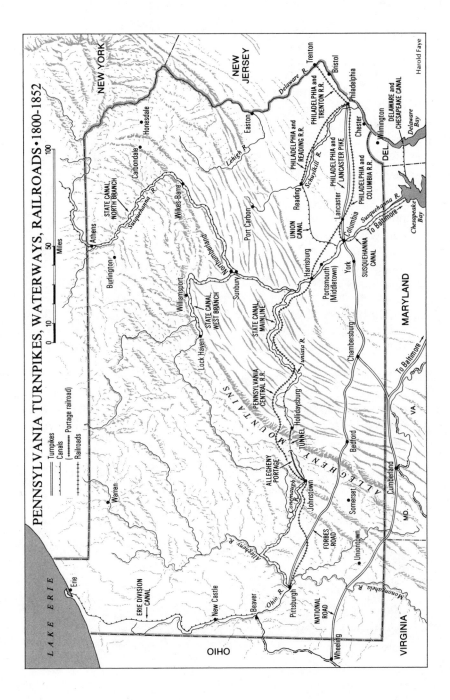

PENNSYLVANIA TURNPIKES, WATERWAYS, RAILROADS · 1800-1852

Turnpikes
Canals
Portage railroad
Railroads

Miles
0   10   50   100

Harold Faye

LAKE ERIE

NEW YORK

NEW JERSEY

MARYLAND

VIRGINIA

OHIO

DEL

Erie

ERIE DIVISION CANAL

New Castle

Beaver

Ohio R.

Pittsburgh

Allegheny R.

Warren

Burlington

Athens

STATE CANAL NORTH BRANCH

Susquehanna R.

Carbondale

Honesdale

Wilkes-Barre

Lehigh R.

Easton

Williamsport

Lock Haven

STATE CANAL WEST BRANCH

Sunbury

Northumberland

Port Carbon

Reading

Schuylkill R.

PHILADELPHIA and READING R.R.

Delaware R.

Trenton

Bristol

PHILADELPHIA and TRENTON R.R.

Philadelphia

Wilmington

DELAWARE and CHESAPEAKE CANAL

Delaware Bay

Chesapeake Bay

Chester

PHILADELPHIA and LANCASTER PIKE

Lancaster

PHILADELPHIA and COLUMBIA R.R.

Columbia

UNION CANAL

Harrisburg

Portsmouth (Middletown)

York

SUSQUEHANNA CANAL

Susquehanna R.

To Baltimore

STATE CANAL MAINLINE

Juniata R.

PENNSYLVANIA CENTRAL R.R.

Hollidaysburg

TUNNEL

ALLEGHENY PORTAGE

Conemaugh R.

Johnstown

FORBES ROAD

Bedford

Chambersburg

Somerset

Uniontown

Cumberland

NATIONAL ROAD

Wheeling

Monongahela R.

To Baltimore

ALLEGHENY MOUNTAINS

MD

VA.

in the case of the Erie Extension, while continuing state plans for improvement. The major such plan at the end of the canal period was a rebuilding of the portage railroad, which by 1853 had cost the state an additional $2,143,000, as compared to only $1,828,000 for its initial construction. Since by then it seemed probable that the Pennsylvania Railroad was to make the portage obsolete, one can only wonder how much such later projects owed to the political connections of construction contractors. Yet, the difficulty in securing subscriptions to the stock of the Pennsylvania Railroad in the 1840s makes it appear highly unlikely that in earlier decades private capital would have financed a railroad across the mountains. The "social" gain would have been great, but the reward in profit to a private company using, let us say, the technology of 1834, would have been very uncertain.

As usual in America, the state system was not the result of a carefully worked out policy or a planned development. It grew from an unco-ordinated series of legislative actions, interrupted from time to time by gubernatorial vetoes. For its part in this system the state had, by 1840, contracted a total debt of $40 million, on which it owed $2 million a year as interest. The burden was not a heavy one for a state with property assessed at $2 billion, but partisan politics prevented adequate taxes during the depression from 1837 to 1843, and to the consternation of the British bondholders, interest payments were defaulted in 1841 and 1842. Ultimately the amounts due were repaid with interest, but meanwhile, because of this and some other state defaults, American governmental credit had suffered greatly. When prosperity returned in the mid-1840s, many English bankers preferred first-mortgage American railroad bonds to state or local securities.

Perhaps never in history has such a great man-made transport system had so short a useful life. Even as the final works were being completed in the middle 1840s, they were being made obsolete by the railroad. Historian of Pennsylvania transportation George Swetnam writes: "By 1860 the Main Line Canal and many of its branches had been sold and were out of business, the highways were unused and overgrown with weeds and brush, and the steamboat industry on the Monongahela and the Ohio was virtually ruined." [1] The brief period of the waterways' strategic importance, scarcely thirty years, has discouraged scholars from undertaking the very difficult task of assessing the economic value of the system. While if the state had put $40 million into properly connected railroads from 1826 to 1845, the results would undoubtedly have been better, the lack of either investment would have had such dire effects that it is inconceivable. For goods shipped from New York to Pittsburgh, the Erie canal to Buffalo plus the connecting canals into Pennsylvania offered lower through rates, but for goods shipped from Philadelphia to Pittsburgh, and even to places in nearby Virginia on the Ohio River, the Mainline was much faster and no more expensive than routing via New York. In addition, the Mainline was ice-free several weeks longer each year than the Erie. Since both the major urban areas of the state were self-sufficient in timber, coal, and iron, the most important and profitable freight was westbound manufactures. Before the railroad reached Pittsburgh in 1852, the canals also provided the quickest and most comfortable passenger routes across the state.

Over the long distances and rough terrain of the United States the triumph of the railroad was inevitable, and, ironically, its successful development in Pennsylvania coincided with the height of canal-building activity. In 1800 the use of transportation by rail was nearly half a century old in the northeastern coalfields of England. For moving stone, coal, or lumber, short lines of track were used in Pennsylvania from 1809 on, and by the 1830s there were many such short lines of up to 20 miles in length. About 1830 the Delaware and Hudson Canal Company tried a British locomotive, the Stourbridge Lion, on its 16-mile road between Carbondale and Honesdale, Pennsylvania, but the engine was too heavy for the track, and the firm continued to use horses.

In 1828 when work had just started on passenger lines in New

---

1. George Swetnam, *Pennsylvania Transportation* (Gettysburg, Pa.: Historical Association, 1968), p. 67.

York, Maryland, and South Carolina, the Pennsylvania legislature authorized construction on the 82-mile Philadelphia and Columbia Railroad as a part of the State Works. By 1832 twenty miles of wooden rails topped by strap iron were opened from Philadelphia west. Only the roadbed and the steam motive power were state owned. Passenger and freight carriages were fitted to the rails by private companies, such as The Pioneer Fast Line, a precursor of many American private car companies, which then paid toll to the railroad. The road originally included a half-mile inclined plane to get up on the plateau at Belmont just west of Philadelphia, and here the state provided assistance with cables run by stationary steam engines. The entire 82 miles to Columbia on the Susquehanna, opened in October 1834, was not a complete solution for east-west shipments. For a decade or more, heavy, bulky products such as coal or lumber overtaxed the power of the engines, and all goods for the west had to be loaded on boats at Columbia. Safety improved when, in 1840, the dangerous strap-iron rails, which could come loose and rise up as "snake heads" through the floors of cars, were replaced by solid iron.

The other important early Pennsylvania railroads were the privately built Philadelphia and Germantown (1834), Philadelphia and Trenton (1838), and Philadelphia and Reading (completely opened in 1839). It is a proof of the slowness of anthracite-coal development that the first eastbound train over the latter road brought 1,635 barrels of flour and only six tons of coal to its Delaware River terminal.

By 1845 the Philadelphia and Columbia had locomotives capable of hauling 75 tons. In contrast one large canalboat (too big for the Union locks) towed by two horses or mules could carry 50 tons, and eventually the Schuylkill Navigation Company had 180-ton boats. Hence the railroad, charging about four cents a mile for a passenger and more than that per ton-mile for freight, was initially for speed rather than economy. But improved locomotive technology, including specialization by both the Baldwin and Norris firms of Philadelphia on different types of engines for passengers and freight, better roadbeds, more gradual curves, and lower grades were all reducing railroad costs, while canal technology stagnated. The event that signaled the final triumph of the steam-powered railroad engine in the state was the chartering of the Pennsylvania Central in 1846.

By 1845 rail lines operated by several private companies connected Buffalo with both Boston and New York City, but no attempt had been made to cross the mountains from Harrisburg to Pittsburgh. A major factor in the delay was the fact that state money was no longer available, and Philadelphia mercantile and financial interests, whose money was essential, were hesitant about investing in such difficult construction. After years of indecision the legislature finally forced action on the easterners by passing a bill stipulating that unless a Pennsylvania railroad company sold $3 million par value of stock and received one million of it in cash by July 30, 1847, an extension of the Baltimore and Ohio to Pittsburgh would be chartered. With aid from interests in the western part of the state that saw the Pennsylvania Central as a better connection to the east, enough Philadelphia investors finally came forward to meet the time requirement. This might be called "state-goaded" rather than "state-assisted" transportation.

Vigorous construction from Columbia up the Susquehanna, west by the valley of the Juniata and across the watershed near the portage railroad completed the Pennsylvania Central connection from Philadelphia to Pittsburgh in December 1852, a few months before the B. & O. reached Wheeling on the Ohio in Virginia and a year after separate lines from Albany to Buffalo had been combined into the New York Central. Five years later the well-managed Pennsylvania Railroad under the leadership of J. Edgar Thomson bought the State Works along the Mainline for $7.5 million, representing, except for part of the roadbed of the Philadelphia and Columbia, largely a payment of tribute to get rid of state competition and regulations, and to gain legislative repeal of the 3-mills-per-mile tonnage tax levied on rail freight.

Except for the initial Philadelphia and Columbia, the spread of railroads within the state was privately financed. In part, this was a matter of timing. The depression from 1839 to 1843 and the resulting interest defaults in the years when railroad building was rapidly expanding led the state to start selling its transportation investments rather than make new ones. Furthermore, mining companies, with no claims on state aid, built the first sections of roads such as the Lehigh Valley Railroad, that ultimately became major links in the eastern rail system. Because the profit was made on the mineral products, return on the cost of the road, per se, was not vitally important. Had this mining use and development of rail technology come earlier, there would probably have been a state-owned trunkline railroad instead of a canal system.

The elements that produced about a $50-million investment in the Pennsylvania State Works, the largest of all American investments in the nineteenth century in planned internal transportation suggest some generalizations applicable to other areas. Geography was primary. Two regions rich in agricultural and other natural resources were under the same political jurisdiction but separated by a substantial mountain barrier. To cross this barrier with economical transport was too large a task for the private capitalists of the early nineteenth century. Gouverneur Morris had said almost exactly this in urging state construction of the Erie Canal in New York to connect the ocean and the lakes. The other states that made early east-west connections either by canal or railroad all had state aid for their initial efforts. Rivalry between Pennsylvania, New York, and Maryland for interior trade was also a factor in producing a hasty authorization of state construction by the legislature at Harrisburg. More generally, seaport rivalry is an impelling force for the government finance of inland transportation. Finally, a factor often overlooked, Pennsylvania in 1826 was probably the richest state, and with adequate fiscal policy the whole investment in public works could be easily absorbed. This suggests the rather obvious conclusion that resources already developed and wealth that could be taxed explain the rapid advance of transportation in the early American industrial areas.

Emphasis on the unique and interesting improvement of transportation within the state should not obscure change and growth in the highly important traffic along the coast. Interregional business, particularly between Philadelphia and New York, grew enormously as imported goods from Europe increasingly reached Philadelphia through the more accessible northern port, and after the late twenties, boatloads of anthracite coal went in the opposite direction. Increasing business is reflected in estimates of the movement of people between the two major cities. In 1790 the figure is set at 10,000 travelers by common carriers in both directions, and in 1840, at 200,000. In 1790 the trip by stage took about 24 hours, by 1840 nearby connecting railroads had reduced the time to under six hours. Unlike the trip to New York, the one to Baltimore in 1790 involved at least one overnight stop and hence took three days. By 1840, partial connection by rail and elimination of any interruption reduced the time to about the same as the trip to New York.[2] The mining and industrial developments that made these speed-ups technologically possible will be the subject of the next chapters.

2. Allan R. Pred, *Urban Growth and the Circulation of Information: The United States System of Cities, 1790–1840* (Cambridge: Harvard University Press, 1973), pp. 158, 178, 180.

6

The Great Home Market

$\mathcal{D}$EMAND was much more important than supply as a maker of change, concludes Diane Lindstrom after an intensive study of the Philadelphia region before 1840.[1] Except for anthracite coal after about 1825, the increases in demand in the Philadelphia market came from growing local population and the rising prosperity of the Pennsylvania backcountry. Put in another way, eastern Pennsylvania was a practically self-sufficient area of industrialization with all the resources necessary in food, labor, and raw materials. Exports of flour, wood, and iron from Philadelphia continued to increase slowly, but anthracite became a rapidly growing regional export. Money from the coal trade both increased demand for local goods and created the foreign exchange needed to buy tropical products, superior manufactures from Europe, and various luxuries.

Improvements in agriculture were a major factor in raising local demand for all manufactured goods. Knowledge and machinery increased productivity and cut man hours of work, so that while food prices declined, the farmer still had a better income. Furthermore, with the construction of canals and hardsurfaced roads more and more farmers were able to sell their products in urban markets or send them to Philadelphia for ex-

---

1. Diane Lindstrom, "Demand, Markets and Economic Development: The Greater Philadelphia Region" (Mss. Ph.D. Thesis, University of Delaware, 1974).

port. Wheat, corn, rye, and oats were grown in all parts of the state, and while the older lands in the east, earlier worn from too continuous cropping, were refertilized and largely used for animal-raising and dairying, these counties were also large producers of corn.

In 1820 the legislature authorized county agricultural societies to spread knowledge regarding fertilization and choice of crops. Using the new ideas, Chester County farmers worked out an eight-to-ten-year plan of crop rotation, which so increased production that it spread to other states as the Chester System. From 1800 on, Robert and Joseph Smith of Bucks County sold superior plows with cast-iron moldboards, which, up to 1835, were confined to the southeastern Pennsylvania and southern New Jersey areas. Major changes in farm equipment and practices generally spread more rapidly after 1840. In the two decades before the Civil War mechanization of agriculture proceeded at a revolutionary rate. Horse-drawn seed drills, harrows, mowers, gang plows, hay rakes, reapers, and threshers came into use. Meanwhile a State Agricultural Society (1851) sponsored over seventy county and local societies that promoted county fairs and other practical demonstrations of new methods. A Farmer's High School of Pennsylvania, opened in 1855, became the Agricultural College of Pennsylvania in 1862.

The rate of increase in demand from the agricultural areas, however, could not approach that of the cities, which grew greatly in size and purchasing power. By 1845 Philadelphia accounted for between a quarter and a third of the assessed value of property in the state, and the expenditures of an urban family were five times greater than those of a farm family.

Philadelphia's continuing position as the major manufacturing city of the nation was based on a wide variety of products. During the entire period between the Revolution and the late nineteenth century the scale of almost all manufacturing operations became larger, and what had been one-man shops, or shops with a master or journeyman and some apprentices, became big enough to be called factories. The causes—advances in technology and greater specialization of tasks—affected different industries in diverse ways. In some, such as leather- or woodworking, small mechanical improvements were continuous; and a shop simply grew larger, dividing its operations more and more without any clear stage at which it became a factory. In some industries, such as window glass or chemicals and drugs, growth was an increasing number of skilled workers brought together in larger plants. The Wetherills, for example, added one chemical and drug process after another to their production and moved from a shop in downtown Philadelphia to a "factory" across the Schuylkill. By 1850 the Board of Trade hailed Philadelphia as the greatest producer of pharmaceutical chemicals in the world. Other operations, such as the manufacture of iron machinery including steam engines, needed large shops with cranes and lathes from the time they began—around 1800. By the 1850s, locomotive makers Baldwin and Norris were each employing hundreds of men.

Textiles have often been regarded as the pioneer factory industries because of the apparently clear line between hand spinning or hand weaving and the same operations done by water-powered machinery. But even here the lines were indistinct. To insure a reliable supply of thread, hand spinners were brought together in factories as early as the 1770s, and after spinning became largely mechanized early in the next century, the weaving of good fabrics, either cotton or wool, was still best done by hand, although many weavers might work under one roof. In Switzerland, a world leader in fine cloth, most weaving was still done by hand in the late nineteenth century. Although Alfred Jenks at Holmesburg, in Philadelphia County, started making textile machinery in 1810, the great strength of Philadelphia in hand weaving delayed mechanization. In Lancaster, the coarse cloth of 1816 was said to be cheaper than that coming from the famous Waltham factory outside of Boston.

As important as technological development or expanding trade was the mature and efficient business structure of the Philadelphia area in finance, distribution, and manufacturing. In manufacturing, the cities along the banks of the Delaware and its tributaries had a very broad mix of processing such as flour milling, meat-packing, sugar refining, distilling, and consumer goods such as textile, carpet, shoe, furniture, and carriage making, as well as general construction, iron processing, shipbuilding, printing and publishing.

The varied business activities of the area employed a large labor force that was mainly of English, German, or Welsh origin. Although people from many other nations could be found among the crowded houses and shops of the metropolis, they were not present in large numbers or discrete communities. Blacks, some filling out their servitude under the gradual emancipation act of 1780, were generally unskilled. Figures for the total number of blacks in Chester and Lancaster counties are available, but not for Philadelphia. Since many of them were more used to country than urban labor, the 3 percent in these two counties in 1800, and the more than 6 percent in 1840, may have exceeded the percentage in the metropolis.

The many skilled craft workers of Philadelphia, chiefly in the printing, shoemaking, tailoring, weaving, and particularly in the building trades, formed some short-lived unions in the 1820s and 1830s. From 1828 on, they also supported labor candidates for local office on coalition tickets with the other parties. The major causes of organized protest by workers seem to have been tighter organization of masters to control wages, long working hours, and governments unwilling to enact laws for general public education or against imprisonment for debt. Both the political and bargaining phases of these movements progressed farthest in Philadelphia before they were ended by the depression after 1837, not to be revived as action groups until the late fifties. These early organizations were in the old crafts only slightly affected, except for textile weaving, by the forerunners of a new industrial order rising around them.

Before a Massachusetts supreme court ruling in 1842 that strike action was legal as long as others' rights or property were not harmed, hostile judicial rulings limited effective direct action to those prosperous times when the busy employer would sooner settle than go to court. While by 1820, judges were willing to concede that unions were legal, they held that the means necessary to make strikes effective, such as picketing, were against the law. Regardless of legal precedents, no factory workers achieved success in collective bargaining before the

Civil War. Wages and hours, as in classic theory, appeared to depend on what would attract and hold an adequate work force.

Dependent on skilled workers and portentous for the transition to modern industrialism in Philadelphia were charcoal iron and crucible steel works, many shops making machinery, and a developing knowledge of practical engineering. Oliver Evans, a self-taught mechanic and inventor born near Newport, Delaware, in 1755, led the way in Philadelphia's rise as an engineering center. His first industrial achievement was the entirely complete mechanizing of water-powered flour milling in the mid-1780s. By the 1790s Delaware Valley flour mills were acclaimed by foreign specialists as the world's best. In 1787 Maryland had given him a patent on the use of steam carriages, but on grounds of safety Pennsylvania had refused. Never able to get financial backing for steam vehicles, he turned to stationary engines and in 1802 installed the first American high-pressure engine in his plant and store in Philadelphia. Between 1807 and his death in 1819, his Mars Iron Works turned out fifty steam engines. But as late as 1816 he failed to get a congressional grant to apply steam to land transportation. The general use of steam, in which Pennsylvania would lead the nation, was still a generation away. Mill mechanics were not competent to keep steam engines in repair, wood was a relatively unsatisfactory fuel for boilers, and consequently improved water power was favored by all but a handful of operators.

"The railway and the steam engine," wrote economic journalist Edwin T. Freedley, "serve to show how truly is the Iron Manufacture the great patron of modern art and industry." [2] But both iron and steam evolved gradually. Most of the early steam engines were used in riverboats; after 1830 a rapidly growing number were used for railroad locomotives. From 1824 on, the Franklin Institute was the nation's chief center of practical engineering knowledge, and its *Franklin Journal and American Mechanics Magazine,* the major periodical. In the 1830s the institute also carried on scientific research. In this

---

2. Edwin T. Freedley, ed., *Leading Pursuits and Leading Men* (Philadelphia: Edward Young, 1856), p. 245.

lively environment it is not surprising that Matthias W. Baldwin and William Norris each started a pioneer locomotive works in Philadelphia in 1832, and that soon their products, designed specially for American conditions, began to replace British imports. The strength of Philadelphia engineering in the 1820s makes the legislature's refusal to build a steam railroad to Pittsburgh seem still more shortsighted.

An initial agent in developing the steam and iron machinery stage of industrialism, the essence of the so-called "revolution," was anthracite coal. This fuel needs certain conditions of continuous draft in order to burn, and then produces previously unprecedented amounts of heat; consequently its commercial use presented many problems. And since wood, even in Philadelphia, was still cheap, most families and manufacturers preferred to use this familiar fuel. Although workable home grates and stoves using coal had been available for over a decade, only 80,000 tons of anthracite left the mining area in 1827. The development of a four-dollar fireplace grate by New Yorkers in 1831 finally put Pennsylvania anthracite on the road to being the chief supplier of heat for northern homes. Meanwhile anthracite from Pennsylvania began to provide an unequaled fuel for eastern iron and machinery industries. After 1840 it became of major importance as a substitute for charcoal in the smelting and forging of iron.

Use of any type of coal for smelting iron was a complicated and little-understood process. Blowing hot instead of cold air into the blast furnace, a process developed for bituminous coal in Scotland in 1828 and for hard coal in Wales in 1837, made the use of anthracite a possibility. But it was two years more before Benjamin Perry from Wales successfully smelted with anthracite at the Pioneer Furnace in Pottsville. As the first anthracite iron poured from the furnace, Nicholas Biddle came from Philadelphia with a five-thousand-dollar award, and at the Mount Carbon Hotel he declared the union of "stove coal" and iron ore to be a second declaration of independence from Britain.

While, from this time on, the use of coal spread rapidly in iron smelting, in 1844 the Philadelphia and Reading Railroad, which served the coalfields, reverted to burning wood. An anthracite fire was too hot for the boilers used in locomotive or stationary steam engines. The railroad found that repair costs on boilers more than ate up the initial saving from using anthracite. So until the 1850s wood-burning locomotives hauled anthracite from the mines. In 1851 and 1852 James Millholland, master of machinery on the Reading, patented new boiler designs suitable for·anthracite, and that road and other local railroads switched to coal. The same improvement, available of course for stationary engines, led to a greatly increased use of steam power.

Thus because of its intense heat, anthracite was initially much more important in reorganizing iron production and in home heating than it was as a source of motive power. With the Millholland boiler, however, the use of anthracite for all purposes was limited only by transportation costs. Most of the nation's long railroads had bituminous somewhere close to the track and it was, therefore, their cheapest fuel. The Pennsylvania Railroad, for example, burned bituminous from 1851 on. Only the roads penetrating the mining area of eastern Pennsylvania burned anthracite. The massive use was for heating homes, offices, and factories in the Middle Atlantic and New England states. In 1820 only 400 tons of anthracite were sent to market from the handful of eastern Pennsylvania counties that contained 99 percent of American hard coal. Forty years later the same counties were marketing 8 million tons, and Pennsylvania as a whole was supplying 80 percent of the nation's coal. The conversion of the northeast to heating by anthracite was in part the result of aggressive promotion by companies such as Lehigh Coal and Navigation and aggressive dealers in Philadelphia. The latter usually had offices in Pottsville and other major coal centers and some owned their own canalboats.

While some coal went directly from the mines to New York City or State over the Delaware and Hudson Canal or Delaware and Raritan Canal, most of it came to Philadelphia by way of the Schuylkill canal system or the Lehigh and Delaware canal system, and made the city the nation's greatest coal port. In the 1850s the Reading Railroad to Philadelphia surpassed the Schuylkill Navigation System in general tonnage, and within a generation railroads led to the abandonment of trunkline canals. Probably the major factor that worked in favor of the rails was time. The coal dealers had much of their working capital tied up in shipments, and the same money could be turned over five or six times as fast when railroads were used. Looked at another way, for the same investment in coal the dealer could receive and sell as much in one day by using the railroad as he could in a week by employing the canal.

But even in 1850 there was still no way of sending heavy goods up and down the coast by rail without costly unloading and reloading between independent carriers. Consequently, the coal not used for heating or manufacturing in the Philadelphia area was shipped by sail to ports from Maine to South Carolina. It was this trade that gave the Port of Philadelphia national supremacy in total outbound tonnage of all types. It also emphasized domestic as against foreign business for Philadelphia merchants. Preoccupied with local shipments of coal, iron, and timber, they had much less interest in European trade than their counterparts in Boston and New York.

While coal dominated midcentury shipments out of Pennsylvania, it was far from the only important raw material. Iron ore lay close to the surface in much of Pennsylvania. Farmers dug ore over fifty percent pure from their fields and took it by wagon to the nearest smelter, usually only a few miles away. Underneath the topmost ore beds were veins of iron running deeply into the hills. One of the richest veins, mined before the Revolution, was at Phoenixville, only some twenty-five miles up the Schuylkill from Philadelphia. Freedley said in 1855, "The Schuylkill, Susquehanna, Allegheny, Juniata, Monongahela and smaller valleys are literally filled with iron." [3] At midcentury Pennsylvania supplied over half the iron ore mined in the United States. Up to that time, the largest developed ore resources were at Cornwall about twenty miles east of Harrisburg, where the Coleman family owned both mines and smelters. As in the colonial period the smelting was done in blast furnaces about forty feet high fired with charcoal, which required both extensive

3. Freedley, *Leading Pursuits*, p. 247.

woodland and many timber cutters. Charcoal iron was the best material for implement makers. Consequently as demand for rolled iron, chiefly for rails, exploded from 1840 on, anthracite smelting for railroad demands grew up alongside the earlier charcoal process but did not replace it.

Iron smelting, refining, and processing is a complicated series of thermochemical actions. Without scientific knowledge of it, the ironmasters could not understand the effects of one stage of treatment on the next. Skilled mechanics in processing plants, for example, failed to realize how much their success in making tools depended on what took place in smelting and refining.

The iron that came directly from the smelting furnace had a high carbon content and impurities such as phosphorus and silicon that made it brittle. Simply poured into molds made of a mixture of clay, loam, and sand, it became pig iron. The pigs might then be taken to a cupola furnace in a foundry, reheated to burn out more carbon and impurities, and then poured into molds with the desired shapes for machine bases, supports used in ships, or for other uses requiring hardness and rigidity but not flexibility or toughness. These operations could be done at the smelting works, but the more usual practice, at least that followed by the Colemans, was to deliver the pigs to Philadelphia iron merchants, such as Cabeen and Company, who would sell them to various types of processors.

The major problems of iron and steel making, none clearly understood until after 1850, were the elimination of sulphur, silicon, and phosphorus contained in the Pennsylvania ore, and very careful regulation of the carbon content. The latter was the factor differentiating all classes of iron and steel from each other. The higher the carbon content, such as 3.5 to 4 percent in pigs from the original blast furnace, the harder and more brittle the iron. The lower the content the more tough and flexible, as in steel that ran from .1 to 1.25 percent carbon. For iron that would be used for tools, shafts, wires, or railroad purposes pigs were reheated to reduce the carbon content to around 2.2 percent. But other impurities also needed to be reduced, and the first step was adding iron oxide to the molten metal and stirring the hot mass in a shallow pit. The stirring was done by men with iron bars; the process was called puddling, and the men were puddlers. Puddled iron still contained some waste compounds, or slag, that would make the product unreliable, and these had to be mechanically eliminated by hammering, squeezing, or rolling the balls of hot metal that came from the puddlers.

The foregoing has been an Olympian view based on twentieth-century knowledge. To the ironmasters of the 1840s or 1850s the treatments were all based on experience with no clear knowledge of what was happening. They knew in a general way, for example, that some steel had less carbon and impurities than wrought (hammered) or rolled iron; but before Henry Bessemer's invention of a new type of furnace or converter in 1857, the masters knew of no inexpensive way to achieve such a degree of purity. They were baffled still more by the way heating caused complex structural changes in the metal; even the most advanced theoretical chemists of the day could not understand that.

Since smelting used more wood or anthracite than iron ore, it stayed in the country close to the sources of fuel. Before the mid-1840s, hammering or rolling was still generally powered by water, so the forges remained along fast-flowing streams. But works for making iron into tools or machines, requiring less power and more skilled labor, were usually located near cities in the first half of the century, particularly around Philadelphia, Harrisburg, and the valley from Coatesville through Lancaster to Columbia on the Susquehanna. While in each of these places fairly good transportation for finished products also played a part, large local markets existed for iron products that were protected from outside competition by a combination of the costs to the outsider of transportation and marketing.

Iron works for stoves, tools, flues, and various fittings were scattered through the old downtown area of Philadelphia from Front to about Sixth or Seventh and from Spruce to Arch streets. The big Baldwin Locomotive Works was further out at Broad and Callowhill, and the Port Richmond area had shipbuilding, iron works, and the Reading Railroad yards. Steam power, spreading in the mid-forties, ended dependence on streams and led owners of mills and forges to seek the better labor supply and marketing resources of the cities. As in the case of the Colemans at Cornwall, this movement led to increasing shipments of pig iron directly to the metropolitan area.

Working capital for the iron industry came largely from Philadelphia merchants. In the days before integrated mills the specialized iron merchants such as Cabeen & Company or Morris and Jones, steered iron through its various stages and sold locally or exported the finished products to American and foreign ports. The same merchants also imported British iron when they had to meet the demands of the complex market that was growing faster than domestic production, or when the price of imported metal was lower, or when special qualities in the metal were needed. So great was the mystery of iron that no one knew exactly why a Swedish iron, for example, was superior for cutting purposes to any of the domestic product.

Rapid construction and equipment of railroads from the 1830s on created a demand for more and stronger wrought or rolled iron than could initially be produced within the state. "Never," say Professors Porter and Livesay, "have so few customers demanded so much material." [4] Efficient production at high temperatures needs to be continuous, and iron merchants were often hard pressed to see that rollers and puddlers received sufficient pig iron with the proper qualities, or that car, locomotive, and rail works had enough of the right type of wrought or rolled iron. Merchants handling the output of furnaces or forges came to ask for guarantees of minimum quantities before advancing credit. To meet the demand American masters, cut off from European knowledge, occasionally reinvented foreign devices and, like the later Japanese, improved upon them in the process. In 1849 John Fritz, for example, invented a mill with three tiers of rollers, already known abroad, that, by having rolls going in both directions, made rolling a continual process while the iron was hot. As we shall see later, a steel-making process similar to Bessemer's was developed at the Cambria

4. Glenn Porter and Harold Livesay, *Merchants and Manufactures* (Baltimore: Johns Hopkins University Press, 1971), p. 80.

Iron Company, in Johnstown, by backwoods ironmaster William Kelly.

Federal tariff laws also changed conditions of competition, particularly for mills rolling rails. The Act of 1842 placed a duty of about 40 percent on "railroad" and other rolled iron. Reduction to 30 percent in 1846 is said to have put severe pressure on American mills, but one suspects that the end of the British railroad boom in 1847 which left British iron works with a large surplus for export, may have been more important in temporarily winning back the American market than was any mild juggling of the tariff. The great American railroad boom from 1850 to 1854 helped to restore Pennsylvania rail making.

Meanwhile cars, wheels, locomotives, and other equipment coming largely from the greater Philadelphia area had more than held their own against foreign competition. Matthias W. Baldwin, pioneer in successful American production of locomotives, illustrates the jack-of-all-trades tradition in American technology. Starting about 1815 to make bookbinding materials, he soon designed the first American rolls for printing cottons, and then adapted his machinery to engraving bank notes. Going on into building hydraulic presses and stationary steam engines, he agreed in 1831 to make a model of a locomotive for Peale's Philadelphia Museum, then in Independence Hall. Convinced from the model that a full-scale railroad engine would be within the capabilities of his shop, he proceeded to build and deliver one to the Germantown Railroad in January 1833. Better suited to light rails, sharp curves, and steep grades than the heavier British imports, but still able to go over 60 miles an hour, Baldwin's locomotive was a success, and he soon received orders for five more. Before the panic of 1837 he had expanded annual production in his plant on Broad Street to nearly fifty locomotives.

William Norris began locomotive building in Philadelphia shortly after Baldwin did, and in the generally flush times through 1836 also succeeded well. Suppliers such as Baldwin and Norris often had to accept payment partially in railroad stock, consequently the depression, which became deepest from 1839 to 1843, halting both completion of roads and the possibility of adequate earnings, put these manufacturers into financial difficulties. Norris was rescued by his brother, a wealthy Philadelphia merchant, and Baldwin, by Asa Whitney, New York railroad builder, who moved to Philadelphia in 1842 and became a partner in the works. Aided by Whitney, Baldwin in the same year developed the "American type" locomotive with a movable front truck and four drive wheels, which, for heavy freight on a track with no extreme curves, could be enlarged to six or even eight drivers. Whitney left his partner and set up his own firm for wheels and other types of railroad equipment, but Baldwin and Norris continued to hold leading positions in the locomotive field. By the mid-fifties Philadelphia produced about three-quarters of the national total of railroad equipment, and both of the leading firms had made over 600 locomotives in plants employing 400 to 500 workers.

In addition to locomotives, wheels, axles, and a multitude of fittings for railroad equipment, Delaware River firms assembled finished cars. Nearly all the early cars were supplied to the Pennsylvania Railroad and the northern Pennsylvania lines by the Philadelphia firm of Kimball and Gorton, the oldest domestic manufacturer. By the 1850s, with a capacity of a thousand cars at one time, the firm was already building passenger coaches with individual reclining seats.

Among the largest users of cast as opposed to wrought iron were the shipbuilders. For a period in the late eighteenth century, Philadelphia had made more ships with larger total tonnage than any other American port, but by the 1840s had fallen behind New York, which had many more local customers. Nevertheless, the Delaware River from Bristol to New Castle had been likened to the famous Clyde Firth and River, center of the great British shipbuilding industry.[5] The screw propeller, which was patented by R. F. Loper and put into ships by Reaney, Neafie and Company at Port Richmond above Philadelphia in the late 1840s, not only required cast-iron bracing, as did sidewheelers, but worked best in an entirely iron ship. Yet, since

---

5. David B. Tyler, *The American Clyde* (Newark, Del.: University of Delaware Press, 1958).

side-wheelers of large size could not pass through the Delaware and Chesapeake Canal whereas propeller boats could, the Delaware River yards, among them the famous William Cramp Shipbuilding Company, launched a large number of wooden propeller ships in the two decades before the Civil War. In the postwar years Charles H. Cramp, the son of the founder, was recognized as a leading innovator in naval architecture. In the sixties he supervised construction of the first compound steam engine in the United States. In the next decade the *St. Louis* and the *St. Paul* from his yard, powered with such engines, captured the blue ribbon for speed in crossing the Atlantic; and two decades later the blowing up of Cramp's finest battleship, the *Maine,* in Havana Harbor led to the Spanish American War.

In the beginning, however, the operators of ocean-going ships paid little attention to iron construction. The pioneer developments were on the rivers and canals. As early as 1825 an iron ship, the *Codorus,* was tried on the Susquehanna but was not commercially successful. The following year the Lehigh Coal and Navigation Company started using iron barges on the eastern Pennsylvania canals. A hundred or more barges were built, mainly at Pittsburgh, during the next decade for use in the west. In the forties Philadelphia shipbuilders started to launch both iron tugs and riverboats. Reaney and Neafie in 1844 claimed to be the first firm to do both hulls and engines in their own yard.

Had the United States continued to subsidize the transatlantic passenger trade after 1857, no doubt such highly developed iron works could have brought an increasing share of the shipbuilding business back to Philadelphia. As it was, the propeller-driven, and all other types of American ocean-going ships were doing poorly in competition with British ships, which enjoyed a number of subsidies, lower wages afloat, and cheaper construction costs. After the middle fifties American sea-going vessels became increasingly confined to the coastal trade in which foreigners were forbidden to compete.

While Philadelphia accounted for nearly half of Pennsylvania's manufacturing output, and in the nation was rivaled only by New York City, Pittsburgh had become a center as completely devoted to business, particularly manufacturing, as any of the leading seaports. Pittsburgh was, in fact, a seaport for the great western river systems. Even after the completion of the Erie Canal to Buffalo, Pittsburgh could supply goods to nearby cities on the rivers more cheaply than could New York. The extraordinary 350 percent growth of Pittsburgh's population from 1830 to 1850, unequaled during these years among leading cities, illustrates the strength of its geographic location.

In assessing the great advantages Pittsburgh enjoyed in water connections, one must keep in mind the early ways of using the rivers. "Navigable" meant that at high water in the spring and early summer, and perhaps in a rainy fall, the normally inadequate depth of the river rose to 8 or 10 feet, and wooden raft-type boats could float downstream, while small steamboats might go in both directions. The mighty Ohio was no exception. The people of Wheeling, about 60 miles southwest of Pittsburgh by land, but 200 miles by river, claimed to be at the head of navigation of the Ohio. But in normal seasons of high water, boats from Pittsburgh readily floated downstream and shallow-draft paddle-wheelers made their way up.

It was true that once every half dozen years or so a drought would stop springtime navigation, and although the channel was gradually improved, there was no systematic deepening of the Ohio until after 1850. Another obstruction to trade in the years of low water was that boat owners favored the largest possible vessels. A big craft could be operated by about the same number of men as a small one, and in normal years the owners of a big boat could make enough extra profit to stand being laid up once in a while. Ice, of course, was the curse of all northern navigation by water, but from this hazard Pittsburgh had several weeks a year more immunity than Buffalo and the Lake Erie area.

The Pittsburgh water connections were not completed until the Cross Cut Canal was constructed from Beaver on the northernmost bend of the Ohio to connect with Youngstown, Warren, Akron, and Cleveland in 1841, and with Erie in 1844, while to the south the Monongahela slack-water system came into full operation in the latter year. This was only eight years before the Pennsylvania Railroad and its connections began to supersede

PENNSYLVANIA

A photographer's essay by Joe Clark, HBSS

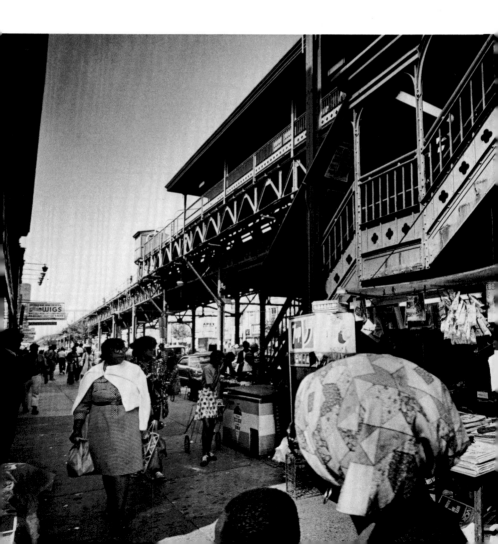

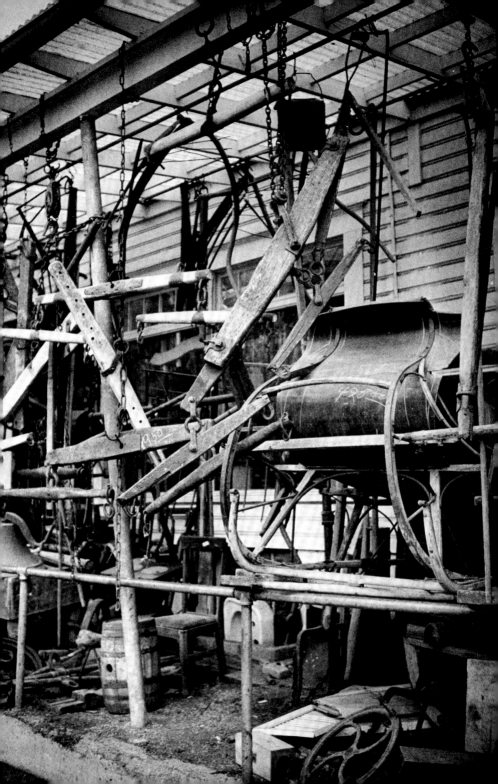

Photos in Sequence

Farm near Allentown.
Golden Triangle, Pittsburgh.
Residential area, Pittsburgh.
Market Street, Philadelphia.
Night in Philadelphia.
Pittsburgh steel mill.
Buggy factory in Lancaster County.
Horse-and-buggy traffic, Lancaster County.
Jeannette cityscape.
Restaurant in Schellsburg.
Remodeled buildings downtown in Philadelphia.
Modern apartment building and Customs House, Philadelphia.
Berean Presbyterian Church in Philadelphia.
Scranton.
Farm near Bird-In-Hand.

the more uncertain waterways as all-year-around carriers of goods. Meanwhile, the new waterways gave Pittsburgh a three-state hinterland for iron products, glass, leather, and textiles.

Wheeling merchants, for example, might ridicule navigation of the river above their city, but they read the Pittsburgh business news and, after the completion of the Pennsylvania state system in 1834, bought increasingly from Pittsburgh merchants. In 1830 this "Gateway to the West" had 15,000 people. In 1850, according to modern census corrections, 68,000. Wheeling, on the other hand, not reliably included in the 1830 census, but perhaps at 4,000 or 5,000 had grown to only 11,000 by midcentury. Along the Ohio Valley the only big city to rival Pittsburgh's growth rate was Cincinnati, which held its early lead reaching an 1850 total of 115,000.

Pittsburgh had grown from the business of her own local area as much or more than from that of the out-of-state western trade. In fact, during the period of most rapid population growth there was little increase in Pittsburgh's goods for export from the local area. Up to 1834, particularly, the Allegheny Mountains and the lack of water transportation from Lake Erie protected Pittsburgh's manufacturing. Only high-priced quality products could stand the freight costs of 5 or 6 cents a pound on goods from the east. Consequently Pittsburgh developed all the types of manufacturing necessary to a self-sufficient community including coarse textiles, leather goods, pottery, furniture, distilling, and iron products. In addition, the local area had excellent clay for glassmaking, from which developed an export industry second only to iron.

The War of 1812 gave temporary stimulation to local western enterprise, but the ensuing depression and better transportation from the east by way of the National Road from Baltimore and the hard-surfaced turnpike to Philadelphia led to some years of stagnation in Pittsburgh manufacturing. The greatest industrial boom of the period before 1850 came in the decade 1826 to 1836. According to local Pittsburgh estimates, whose undoubted bias may have been uniform, iron manufacture rose from a value of $1.2 million to about $6 million; glass from $.2 million to $1.3; textiles $.3 million to $.6; and gunsmithing from $.2

million to around $5 million. Due to precipitous declines in the long depression from 1837 to 1843, the 1836 figures were not approximated again until 1850, although the city was more than twice as populous. This not only suggests that new boom areas were more sensitive to the business cycle than older centers, but also lends support to the thesis that, with greatly increasing water-borne trade from 1834 on, Pittsburgh temporarily became more commercially oriented and proportionately less industrial.

Another explanation of the check to industrial development may lie in the problems that held back the western iron industry: high costs for transportation before the railroad and failure to perfect coke smelting that could make use of the nearly continuous beds of bituminous coal. Only in the decade after 1860 were iron and steel to make Pittsburgh the world center of their production.

Meanwhile, the growth of population and commerce was reflected in the rise of financial institutions. The first bank in Pittsburgh, a branch of the Philadelphia-based Bank of Pennsylvania, opened in 1803. In 1817 this same office also became a branch of the Second Bank of the United States. By the prosperous middle twenties Pittsburgh had two more chartered banks and the first private banker in the western part of the state, Nathaniel Holmes. These plus a second private bank in 1830 and a savings bank in 1834 remained the financial houses of the city up to 1850.

Insurance was supplied before the 1830s by branch offices of eastern firms, but by the end of the boom in 1837 there were three local companies. Marine casualty was a greater risk on the treacherous shallow rivers than on the ocean, and at least one local banking company had given it up after a trial. Fire insurance also grew slowly. Of an estimated $2 million in damage inflicted by the great Pittsburgh fire of 1845, only $700,000 was covered by insurance. The fact that within a short time the companies were able to meet the claims is said to have given a great boost to such insurance in the western region.

By 1850, as railroad building increased at unprecedented rates, particularly in the Middle West, Pittsburgh had resumed its progress toward greatness in iron manufacture. Thirty foundries were turning out pig iron and castings, while thirteen additional mills were rolling sheets and rails. Altogether over 5,000 men were employed, and the product was valued at $6.5 million. While, like iron, glass at a value of $1 million had only about equaled the production rate of 1836, textiles were recorded as having increased 200 percent to an 1850 value of $1.5 million. These mid-nineteenth-century census figures are far less reliable than those of a century later, but they present the picture of a well-established and growing industrial community.

The growth both economically and in population of the state as a whole had gone through two rather distinct periods. During the first, profits from ocean trade and the growth of seaboard mercantile institutions had been dominating factors. New York State had outstripped Pennsylvania; river steamboats had opened a large hinterland for trade through New York City, and New York, of course, was more accessible for all types of ocean-going vessels than was Philadelphia. In the period from about 1830 to 1850, the Pennsylvania inland empire of coal, iron, and lumber began its rapid growth, outdistancing upper New York State, which had much less raw material. Specifically, Pennsylvania in 1810 had been more populous than New York; by 1830 New York had become 42 percent larger, but by 1850 New York's margin over Pennsylvania in population had fallen to 34 percent, and the trend was to continue for the rest of the century. The often belittled Pennsylvania state works in canals and river improvement had much to do with the rapid growth after 1830. Though not the best system possible at the time, the waterway system opened the inland empire. It prepared the way for growth during the following decades when the completion of the Pennsylvania Railroad, the successful adaptation of coke from western coal to smelting iron, and the discovery of the uses of oil were to launch the state on its greatest phase of economic development.

7

The Inland Empire: Energy

*T*HE period of industrialization that can be called revolutionary, the one in which rather simple wooden machinery was replaced by mechanically controlled iron and steel devices, in which railroad and telegraph bound the nation into one market, in which modern chemical knowledge became commercially useful, and in which oil and electricity were first applied to industry, ended around 1890. Although electricity, petroleum, and the internal-combustion engine were to make great changes from then on, these were improvements to major processes already mechanized. The resources of greatest value to Pennsylvania during the more revolutionary period were anthracite and bituminous coal, and the most valuable products those made of iron or steel, but in the last decades of the great change oil produced some of the major business struggles and much public excitement.

Better illumination was an immediate challenge to technologists in the 1850s. By midcentury there were nearly sixty urban gas plants that demonstrated the value of more light, but gas lines were necessarily limited to thickly built up areas, at a time when most people lived in the country. Of the various oils for lamps, each had its disadvantages. Whale oil, which burned safely and brightly, was expensive; camphine, distilled from turpentine, was also bright but readily exploded; oil produced by distillation from coal, while relatively cheap, gave poorer light than the other oils. Because of its low cost, however, coal oil was the most widely used. Hence there was a strong demand for a better kind of lighting oil, and there were coal-oil plants capable of producing it through new and complex distilling processes.

From early in the century, petroleum, known as rock oil, had appeared as an unwanted by-product of drilling for salt wells. Water in salt wells brought up a brine, from which salt was obtained through evaporation. In 1839, at Tarentum in Allegheny County, Thomas Kier struck at a depth of 465 feet, both the wanted brine and a troublesome amount of unwanted oil. For over five years he dumped the oil into the state canal, but then his son Samuel M., a canalboat operator who had seen "Indian" or "Seneca" oil sold in stores, decided that this fluid seemed similar enough to be sold in bottles. Erecting a bottling plant in 1849 Samuel put on a great local marketing drive for oil as the universal panacea for aches and pains, at a dollar a pint. Although selling costs ate up most of Kier's profits, the campaign suggested to men interested in lighting the existence of a possible new source for illuminating oil.

Even after a Yale professor, Benjamin Silliman, Jr., analyzed the liquid for some New Haven businessmen and reported in 1855 that distillation by existing methods would yield 50 percent in good illuminating oil, no one knew whether a large enough supply could be relied upon for commercial promotion. Until such a supply at low cost was assured, the coal-oil distillers would not convert their plants. The only men who took a continuing active interest were some small capitalists in New Haven and New York City, without adequate funds for exploration involving unknown locations and processes of recovery. The men who could profit most from discovery of major sources of oil were the large owners of timberland in western Pennsylvania, and they also were the ones with the most knowledge of what was going on. But lumber owners and dealers such as Brewer, Watson & Company of the Titusville area, were content to let others take the experimental risks.

In 1857 the New Haven and New York group, through its Pennsylvania Rock Oil Company, sent Edward L. Drake, a retired railroad conductor, to drill on land leased from Brewer, Watson, and Company at Titusville. The spot for drilling was selected because oil was oozing from low-lying ground, but it took Drake, who was unfamiliar with both the area and the men in the drilling business, nearly two years to find a properly qualified driller. Finally, on August 28, 1859, just as funds from the east were running out, W. A. ("Uncle Billy") Smith, the driller, struck oil. Before news of the strike could reach George Bissell of the Pennsylvania Rock Oil Company in New York City, Jonathan Watson of the local lumber firm was riding from farm to farm securing drilling rights from his friends among the rather poor German and Irish farmers of the area. There was plenty of land, however, for all the small capitalists interested, because the supply problem was still not solved. One pumped well, remote from transportation and located without any geological knowledge of the area or even any other wells being nearby, was insufficient to warrant conversion of large coal-oil distilling plants.

For two years the increasing production from wells in Venango County from Titusville south to Oil City, more than a hundred miles north of Pittsburgh, failed to interest either eastern distillers or railroads. While the Pennsylvania Rock Oil Company built a barrel factory at Franklin on the Allegheny River, and oil could be floated by barge to Pittsburgh, where Samuel Kier and Charles Lockhart built early refineries, the supply on a national basis was still small. Then, near the confluence of Oil Creek and the Allegheny River, on April 17, 1861, Henry Rouse struck a 3,000-barrels-a-day flowing well.

Now there was little doubt about enough oil under western Pennsylvania to work a revolution in lighting, and the business world became attentive. In 1861 the railroad stations nearest the Venango fields were about 25 miles away, at Corry in Erie County and Garland in Warren; both were on the Sunbury and Erie Railroad, which terminated at Garland. From there the Cleveland, Plainsville and Ashtabula Railroad connected with both the New York Central Railroad and the Erie Railroad to the east and the Lake Shore and Michigan Southern Railroad to the west. At Pittsburgh the Pennsylvania Railroad ran eastward, and its affiliate, the Pittsburgh and Fort Wayne, westward. Another road, the Cleveland and Pittsburgh, intersected the P. and F.W. at Rochester, near the western border of the state. The Pennsylvania promptly leased the Sunbury and Erie (renaming it the Philadelphia and Erie), so that initially the PRR had control of rail transportation from the fields in all directions. The Erie Railroad, running to New York, moved in, however, by extending its subsidiary, the Atlantic Great Western, to Corry in 1861 and later to Franklin on the Allegheny River. Meanwhile, the Pennsylvania bought control of the Oil Creek Railroad from Corry to Titusville, and extended the Philadelphia and Erie eastward to connect with other lines owned or controlled by the Pennsylvania system.

Recounting this network as of 1865 gives a misleading picture of the efficiency of transportation facilities. Only the New York Central and the Pennsylvania had the "standard" four-foot-eight-and-a-half-inch gauge or width of track. Even the Pennsylvania-controlled Pittsburgh and Fort Wayne had four-foot-ten gauge, as did the Cleveland, Plainsville and Ashtabula, while the Erie and the Atlantic Great Western had six-foot gauge. Even north from Philadelphia to New York the four-foot-ten-gauge Camden and Amboy Railroad and Philadelphia and Trenton Railroad both lacked direct rail connections with the Pennsylvania. Hence oil transportation required much cartage and reloading.

The location of refineries was linked more to special railroad rates than to proximity of the fields. Since the products of distilling and refining were all used for lubricants and other purposes as well as illuminants, there was little loss in bulk during the process. In other words, refining could take place wherever labor was plentiful and bargaining power with the railroads was high—either at a sizable city located near the fields and served by competing railroads, or at the chief east-coast ports, close to large domestic and export markets. Cleveland in the west had direct connections to the fields and strong rail, lake, and canal competition both eastward and westward. In the east, New York and Philadelphia were the logical centers. This is the pattern that was finally established, but only after two decades of business drama.

Several heroic figures entered into the contests between cities, refiners, and railroads, Cornelius Vanderbilt and Jay Gould among them, but the two most important actors were John D. Rockefeller and Thomas A. Scott. Scott was a western Pennsylvanian born in 1823 at Fort Loudon, south of Pittsburgh. With little formal education, he had most of his early business experience on the state transportation system. His career on the Pennsylvania Railroad roughly coincides with the rise of oil production and also with that of the organization of the eastern railroad trunklines. He became general superintendent of the Western Division centered at Pittsburgh in 1858, and in 1860 he became the railroad's first vice-president.

Scott's rise was aided by the friendship of J. Edgar Thomson, president of the road. The quick, imaginative, and charming Scott, who impressed everyone with his business ability, was the opposite of the quiet, precise, literal-minded Thomson, an engineer who generally avoided public appearances. Yet, beneath his rather austere, conservative surface, Thomson was apparently fascinated by Scott's bold schemes, and usually he took a part in them. Scott would no doubt have pushed ahead more rapidly in forming a unified Mississippi Valley–Atlantic Coast trunkline, had he not served as chief of the Union's railroad operations during the Civil War, an activity that led him to leave Andrew Carnegie in charge of the Pennsylvania's Western Division. It was during these war years that the Pennsylvania finished the Philadelphia and Erie and two shorter railroads to the oilfields. The railroad situation in Pennsylvania, however, has to be seen in the light of the larger plans of Scott and Thomson, and of the pressures on the Pennsylvania Railroad.

After the war Scott and Thomson, working more as partners than as vice-president and chief executive, built up a railroad empire that by 1880 had made the Pennsylvania Railroad, with 30,000 employees and $400 million in capital, the world's largest corporation. The first postwar step was purchase of complete control of the lines west of Pittsburgh by 1868, and two years later these were vested in a new subsidiary called the Pennsylvania Company. In 1871 the unsatisfactory connection to New York was rectified by the Pennsylvania leasing and rebuilding the United Canal and Railroad Companies of New Jersey. At the same time, leases gave the Pennsylvania complete control of the route to Baltimore and Washington.

Scott led Thomson into personal plans for a transcontinental system, but the plans never matured satisfactorily. From 1871 to 1872 Scott was president of the Union Pacific Railroad, but the partners lacked faith enough in the future of the road to resist a chance to sell their holdings in 1872 at a considerable profit. This enabled the Gould interests to take control of the board and put in their own management. Similarly a venture that made Scott president of the unfinished Texas Pacific Railroad from 1872 to 1880 led to large personal losses for the investors and never culminated in acquisition by the Pennsylvania.

During these years the PRR was largely preoccupied with buying and leasing southern lines in the Atlantic coastal states, so that quite aside from the western plans of Scott and Thomson, the directors were busy dealing with larger problems than the local transportation of oil.

Of both Scott and Thomson it may be said that under the restraining influence of the directors of the Pennsylvania, they managed the PRR finances better than their own. Since no company ever set up a unified national system, it seems reasonable to conclude that the managerial and competitive difficulties were too great to make such a far-flung, complicated venture profitable; but the Pennsylvania could have entered such a plan with more hope of success than any other railroad.

In any contest involving resources within the state, the Pennsylvania Railroad had a political advantage. From the victory of Simon Cameron as both United States senator and political boss of Pennsylvania at the end of the Civil War, the state was controlled for over fifty years by Republican political czars friendly to business. While it was said by a contemporary wit that the Standard Oil Company had done everything possible to the legislature of Pennsylvania except to refine it, the joke depends more on word play than truth. By the 1870s the oil company had a strong lobby, but the major influence on legislation was that of the Pennsylvania Railroad, and particularly Tom Scott. In 1868, for example, the legislature granted a series of special holding-company charters, many for nonexistent firms known as Tom Scott's companies, one of which was to materialize and play a major role in the struggle for the control of oil.

The other leading figure in giving structure to the petroleum industry, John D. Rockefeller, possessed a most unusual mixture of the abilities needed for business success. Save for a demeanor that, from an early age radiated mature wisdom from penetrating eyes, there was little outwardly unusual about Rockefeller. He was slender, medium-sized, and retiring. He made decisions based on careful calculations and preferred to have other men carry them out. Perhaps his rarest quality was his willingness to share power with men he regarded as able and reasonable. He never held a controlling interest in Standard Oil, yet was always the acknowledged leader on the basis of his understanding.

By the end of the Civil War, Rockefeller had formed a small Cleveland partnership for oil refining. In the fields there were now scores of producers who suffered from overproduction, and a smaller, better organized group of refiners, still chiefly located around Pittsburgh. The trend of the industry seemed clearly toward continued oversupply of oil, cut-throat competition, and minimal profits. In England or France binding trade agreements might have been made between the producers. In Germany or Japan the government would have assisted in setting up cartels or Zaibatsus, but in the United States the courts held any agreements to quota production or to fix prices as conspiracies in restraint of trade. Hence if the industry was to be organized on a profitable basis, the action had to be taken by some indirect private means.

In the period up to 1871, the railroad executives sought, at least, to insure some profits for their companies from transporting the oil, and Scott also wanted to protect the western Pennsylvania refiners in the interest of his own road. In 1866 a third meeting of the three trunklines produced a rate agreement, but since both the Pennsylvania and the New York Central owned separate freight-carrying companies, basic rail rates were not a decisive factor.

The Empire Transportation Company was the Pennsylvania's freight subsidiary. In 1865 it took a step forward in technology by building a five-mile pipeline to transfer oil from Pithole on the Allegheny River to the Oil Creek Railroad. In a few years all important "gathering" was done by pipelines at a fraction of the cost of carting. In 1868 Empire introduced the present-day horizontal boiler-type tank cars, made necessary in 1871 by a New York State safety act against railroad transportation in upright tanks.

As the operating head of the railroad most involved with the problems of the industry, Scott, after conferences with both leading refiners and the trunklines, brought forward the South Improvement Company plan. It was essentially a trade association agreement designed to achieve regulation without violation of the law. In the plan the leading refiners in the major cities were selected as the logical organizing group. They would be asked early in 1871 to buy shares in a specially chartered Pennsylvania holding company designed by Scott's lawyers. From the railroad's standpoint the quotas proposed by the directors of this company represented a reasonable division of oil traffic: 45 percent to the Pennsylvania, and 27½ percent each to the Erie and the New York Central; the latter by then controlled the route through Cleveland to the west. Secret rates were designed that, while giving the roads their normal return, would penalize refiners who, because of the terms offered, refused to join the South Improvement Company. The advantage, in the form of high posted rates and rebates given to the S. I. members on all oil shipped, was so great that ultimately all but small refiners with a local business would have been forced to join. Within the company the Philadelphia and Pittsburgh refiners divided control about evenly with those of Cleveland. The refiners that might have to be forced in were located in the oil regions, New York City, and other sea and lake ports. In defense of their independence the refiners in the oil regions helped to form the Petroleum Producers' Union, which attacked the S. I. through the Pennsylvania legislature and won repeal of its charter, as well as the passage of a law that insured independent transportation by giving pipelines local rights of eminent domain.

For the next half-dozen years other attempts were made by the largest refiners, particularly those in Rockefeller's Standard Oil group, by the railroads, and by important producers to control sagging prices, to reduce overproduction, and to end transportation rate wars. In all of these attempts both Rockefeller and Scott appear to have been working for profit through good organization that would include anyone willing to join with them on what they regarded as a reasonable basis.

One of the factors that defeated all attempts at voluntary limitation of production was continuous spread of the fields. Between Oil City and Pittsburgh a southern region opened. To the north around Bradford and on across the New York border production reached new heights in the late seventies, and finally an oil region running into West Virginia was discovered in Washington and Green counties. Each field brought new producers, often with lower costs, who could break any existing voluntary agreement.

Meanwhile both Scott and Rockefeller had their companies build pipeline connections to the coast, and S.O. secretly bought refineries in Pittsburgh and Philadelphia. In the transportation battle the Pennsylvania, with its superior pipeline connections, was getting ahead of the New York Central and the Erie. While the situation between S.O. and the PRR was essentially unstable, it might have been maintained except for the extreme pressures of the long depression from 1873 to 1878. When the Pennsylvania executives went into refining by having their Empire Transportation Company buy plants in New York City and Philadelphia in 1877, Standard Oil withdrew its business from the road. The most unmanageable factor separating the two companies was the control of pipelines. In entering this business on a trunkline basis by building along the Erie right-of-way to New York City, the Rockefeller group had entered the field of long-distance transportation. Scott's group countered by buying refineries.

Just as the great battle of the Pennsylvania, Empire, and the independent refiners against S.O. was joined, the railroad strikes of 1877 delivered a telling blow. Damage from riots reached a maximum on the Pennsylvania at Pittsburgh, and the road was faced with difficulty in maintaining its dividends. As a result Scott agreed to a compromise, which abandoned the railroad's support of the independents. Empire sold its refineries and gathering lines to S.O. and its rolling stock to PRR, which paid for it with money borrowed from S.O. By 1878 Standard Oil controlled 90 percent of the nation's refining capacity, but division of the business between states in local subsidiaries, such as S.O. of Ohio or Indiana, made any antitrust action by a state seem unpromising.

In spite of the anguish caused to many of the refiners and producers of Pennsylvania, S.O. may well have hurt them no more in the long run than would continued cut-throat competition that would have made the business unprofitable and quickly have driven out the weak. By 1877 S.O. was a large exporter, and its principal competition was Russian and Roumanian. The combine could reduce costs by economies of scale, improved technology, and cheap transportation to a degree impossible for small firms. If, of course, the smaller operators could have formed a binding cartel, they might have accomplished these economies to some extent, but this was forbidden by the decisions of both state and federal courts. With the advantage of hindsight it appears that, given the uniform interpretation of the common law by the courts, either a few large companies or the trunkline railroads, or both, were bound to secure most of the profit.

From the standpoint of the development of the state, the oil wars had built up the Philadelphia area as a coastal refining center second only to Bayonne, near New York City, while Cleveland had superseded Pittsburgh for the western business. By 1883 Pittsburgh had only one refinery. In 1884 the Pennsylvania Railroad's successful opposition to a state grant of eminent domain for through pipelines paid off, when Standard Oil settled with PRR for 26 percent of the charges for all shipments by pipeline to the east coast in return for the privilege of crossing the railroad's right-of-way. By then the greatest period of Pennsylvania oil had already been reached. In 1889 the highly productive Lima fields in Ohio became commercially useful, and from 1890 on, Pennsylvania's importance gradually declined, although as late as 1900 the state still produced sixty percent of the nation's oil.

Natural gas, a by-product of drilling for oil, had been allowed to escape in the early days, but by 1870 the supply from wells became so large and continuous that cities such as Pittsburgh used it for heating and lighting. At Rogers and Burchfield's iron works in Armstrong County, in 1874, gas supplied all the fuel required for puddling, heating, and steam power. By the next decade gas was becoming the usual fuel for Pennsylvania iron and steel manufacture. The state remained the largest producer of both oil and natural gas until the great southwestern oilfields were opened up in the early twentieth century.

Exploitation of the immense coal resources of the state has two separate but overlapping histories. Anthracite in the east had a period of great importance for iron making, but in the long run it became primarily a clean heating fuel. Western Pennsylvania bituminous could also be used for both purposes, but its irreplaceable use was for making coke with which to produce iron. Nowhere else in the nation was there any comparable supply of coking coal. About a third of the state's 45,000 square miles had bituminous coal beneath the surface. But smelting with coke encountered numerous technical difficulties, and not until the mid-1870s did it overtake the use of anthracite in the iron industry. Meanwhile hard coal had become the standard fuel for household heating in the northern states.

In contrast to some 15,000 square miles of Pennsylvania bituminous coal land, practically all of the nation's anthracite has come from a northeastern section of the state, covering no more than 500 square miles. There were four distinct collections of veins: a large northern one in Lackawanna and Luzerne counties that served to build up the cities of Wilkes-Barre and Scranton; probably larger and certainly deeper southern deposits around Pottsville in Schuylkill County; a smaller middle region immediately to the north running from the city of Mahanoy to Shamokin in Schuylkill and Cumberland counties; and finally a middle eastern field in Luzerne and Carbon counties centered around Hazleton. That Scranton, close to the northern end, is only fifty some miles from Pottsville near the southern end, shows the close proximity of all the "regions." The northern field had shallow deposits around 1,000 to 1,200 feet that were the most completely exploited in the late nineteenth century. The southern field with its largest deposits at depths approaching a mile, was responsible for most of the 10,000 tons of anthracite still mined in 1970. The annual value of anthracite ranged from $60 million to $90 million in the late nineteenth century, averaging well over twice the value of oil, and production continued to expand to a production of 90,000 tons worth some half-billion dollars in 1920.

From a business standpoint the two sources of energy, anthracite coal and oil, had important features in common: in the period before 1880 they were both extracted from a limited area in Pennsylvania by many independent producers who could readily flood the market; in both cases railroad transportation, partly controlled by out-of-state companies, was used as a factor for control of prices and production, and both resources were exploited by New York as well as Pennsylvania capitalists. The major differences were that unlike oil, anthracite had only a small export market, needed no refining, and could not be shipped by pipeline. The history of the slow and uncertain building of the control of anthracite production by eight competing railroads emphasizes the importance of the Standard Oil group of refiners as effective organizers.

Initially the Philadelphia and Reading Railroad dominated the southern field where it carried coal produced by independent mining firms. Content with the situation, the railroad lobbyists at Harrisburg maintained, until 1869, a law forbidding railroads from conducting mining. Meanwhile three railroads—the Central of New Jersey, the Lehigh Valley, and the Delaware, Lackawanna and Western—all chiefly financed through New York City, had come into the middle and northern fields often in alliance with mining companies, such as Lackawanna Iron and Coal, and had become large owners of coal lands. Three other railroads—the Erie, the Ontario and Western, and the Delaware and Hudson—were also competitors for out-of-state shipments. The Pennsylvania Railroad initially preferred to work with the Reading and the Central of New Jersey rather than to invade the area competitively with its own tracks. In 1869 the state legislature, dominated by political boss Simon Cameron, was induced by both the local and New York interests to repeal the ban on mining by railroads. Campaigns by the transportation companies to buy producers immediately followed. The difference between the policies of the railroads and those of Standard Oil was that no one of the most interested roads was strong enough financially to dominate the situation during the early years and to bring about compulsory mergers.

Following repeal of the restraining act, the Reading bought extensively in the southern region, thus joining the three other well-established anthracite roads who through subsidiary companies were already major coal producers. While the new state constitution of 1874 included a prohibition on mining by railroad companies, it was not effective in separating the subsidiary or controlled companies from their parents. Railroad-rate pools had much the same history as in the case of oil. Started in 1872, pools only succeeded tolerably well in the prosperous years 1879 to 1884. The use of pipelines had largely eliminated railroads from the oil business by 1884, but they still controlled anthracite shipments. Efforts by Reading president, Franklin B. Gowen, to merge the coal roads into a single company failed from both lack of cash resources and the hostility of the firm of Drexel, Morgan and other investment bankers. Between 1880 and 1894 the Reading was forced to undergo three receiverships, which ended with Drexel, Morgan virtually in control.

That turned out to be the ultimate solution. Through the financial influence of J. P. Morgan and Co. (renamed following A. J. Drexel's death in 1893) the major coal-owning railroads were held to effective agreements, even though pooling had been forbidden by the Interstate Commerce Act of 1887. The Temple Iron Company, a Pennsylvania holding company, made the allotments, and each road "unfailingly adhered to its percentage allowance." [1] The harmony depended on interlocking directorates, defined by J. Pierpont Morgan as a community of in-

1. William Z. Ripley, *Railroads: Finance and Organization* (London: Longmans, Green, 1915), p. 546.

terest, which after 1901 included the Pennsylvania Railroad, as new owner of the Jersey Central. The few independents, chiefly in the diminishing northern field, were paid a price equal to 65 percent of that received by the railroads at tidewater.

The histories of anthracite and oil illustrate two means by which competing companies achieved orderly production and prices in spite of the severe common-law restraints on conspiracy, and, after 1890, a federal antitrust law. Whether the public or the State of Pennsylvania would have benefited from unrestrained competition is impossible to tell. There are no exact analogies. In all other nations reasonable agreements between competitors were either accepted by the courts or initiated and enforced by governments. Controlling the supply in the case of coal was beneficial because of the loss by "rust" or oxidation when large banks of unsold coal had to be carried over from one season to the next. The argument that the retail price of anthracite was kept too high may be answered by the fact that it was a rapidly exhausting and irreplaceable resource in the use of which efficiency should have been forced either by effective controls or by the market device of high prices.

In both histories the state ultimately lost most of these resources in less than a century and a half, and with the resource loss went a substantial part of the commonwealth's early economic supremacy. Much the same thing (as will be seen in the next chapter) happened with iron ore, which today comes largely from the west and foreign sources, but bituminous coal turned out to be such an extensive resource that after more than a century of active exploitation, Pennsylvania and adjoining West Virginia and Kentucky are still the major producers.

While bituminous coal lies barely beneath the topsoil in many of the western counties, it was little used before 1840. Timber was not only an early source for heating and iron making, but cutting it opened up more farmland. Raw bituminous burned with a smoky flame, and was generally too sulphurous for use in blast furnaces. Its use for heating homes was also discouraged by the smell of sulphur compounds. In any case, at this period most of the iron was produced east of the mountains.

In Britain in the eighteenth century John Cort had demonstrated that when bituminous coal was heated for a considerable time in the absence of air, the volatile elements such as sulphur were eliminated. At first this was done by covering the coal with earth and then heating it by a flue, but soon ovens were devised that derived much of their heat from burning the gases emitted from the coal. Known as beehive because of the domed shape of the combustion area, they became the standard coke ovens of the nineteenth century. In later years by-product coke ovens separated tar, ammonia, and other valuable products, and then burned the residual gas in flues rather than over the coal itself.

The difficulties in making coke were not great. The problem was to find coal that made coke suitable for smelting iron, and then to readjust the smelting-furnace process. Several early attempts to copy British methods failed. One in 1824 at Farrandville on the West Branch of the Susquehanna in Clinton County, with equipment from Scotland, is said to have lost its backers the immense sum of half a million dollars. A decade later the Franklin Institute was still offering a prize for commercially workable smelting with coke. The first success came at Lonaconing, across the border in Maryland, but continuous coke production in Pennsylvania began from two beehive ovens built on the farm of John Taylor on the Youghiogheny River south of Connellsville in Fayette County. They produced coke late in 1841, thereby helping to initiate the most important change in the iron industry before the introduction of Bessemer steel.

Since not all bituminous is good coking coal, and the beehive process required knowledge and experience, the spread of the use of coke was slow. Furthermore, coke was competing in the western area primarily with charcoal, which was much better understood as a smelter fuel, still cheap to procure, and made good, reliable iron for farm uses and machinery. In the east, although anthracite needed no purification for use in smelting, and produced reliable pig, it did not surpass charcoal until 1855, and in the 1870s there were still nine charcoal-burning iron furnaces within forty miles of Philadelphia. Not until 1869 was more pig iron made in the state from coke than charcoal and not until 1875 more from coke than from anthracite. It was found, however, that a mixture of coke and anthracite worked better than either fuel alone.

Ultimately, as both eastern anthracite and ore increased in price, and entrepreneurs such as Henry Clay Frick developed cheap coke, it superseded all other fuels in smelting, reaching 98 percent in the first decade of the twentieth century. The nation's one large source of good coking coal was western Pennsylvania; the state continued to produce more coke than all other states combined, with Connellsville as the center of the industry.

It was this natural or regional monopoly that kept iron processing in the Pittsburgh area. Local iron ore was running out, and Lake Superior ore was preferred for steel, but about two tons of coal were required to smelt one ton of ore, and hence all the vast array of smelters, converters, and mills were tied to coking coal rather than ore. In spite of a considerable dispersion of steel making and also glassmaking over the United States east of the Mississippi, Pennsylvania retained its primacy in production of both because of coal.

That industrially mature Pennsylvania in the twentieth century has close rivals in coal and iron production, and that some newer steel-consuming industries such as automobile and truck manufacturing are located elsewhere, is, of course, a benefit to the nation as a whole. But in the half-century from 1840 to 1890 there was no substitute for Pennsylvania. Had this central area of resources and skills not existed, had there been no American Clyde along the Delaware, no centers of machinery manufacture around Chester and Philadelphia or no steel concentration around Pittsburgh, American progress in the heavy-industry stage of industrialization would have been far slower, perhaps slow enough to keep the nation of the nineteenth century primarily agricultural.

8

The Inland Empire: Manufacturing

$\mathcal{W}$HILE the natural resources in mines and forests and the strategic location of Pennsylvania were basically responsible for the rapid industrialization of the nation between 1840 and 1890, only the usable finished products, of course, counted as social gain. And these depended not only on cheap materials but even more on high levels of mechanical skill that had been developing since the early eighteenth century. The progress also indicates that while natural resources may give a particular emphasis to the adoption of new technology, as in steel making, the developing complex produces new supplies of workers and entrepreneurs who find ways of seizing the possibilities for ever more numerous employment and avenues to business profits.

Hence, while Pennsylvania's essential contribution was in coal and iron, the state also led the nation, at one time or another during the last half of the nineteenth century, in the production of glass, leather goods, timber and wood products, cement, machinery, ships, and textiles. In some types of manufacturing its rivalry with other states was close, as with various types of textiles, chemicals, and ships, and in timber cutting, where leadership might shift each decade; but in leather goods, machinery, glass, and the total yardage of textiles, Pennsylvania retained steady leads, approaching its supremacy in the basic production of oil, coal, and iron.

Glassmaking was dependent on sources of silicon and cheap

fuel, both of which were found around Pittsburgh from the early part of the nineteenth century. In spite of high tariff duties, British competition held back glassmaking in the east, but the difficulty of sending glassware—even by canal and rail—over the mountains afforded the western producers high protection. After 1850 the western industry advanced rapidly with the help of a growing western market and a better supply of skilled technicians. For the decade 1850 to 1860 the total rate of increase in glass production in Pennsylvania was around 80 percent. By 1870 the state produced over half of the nation's glass. It was an exotic industry largely dependent on the skill of methodical German technicians—who were highly secretive about formulas—and on their experience in handling the successive stages of heating the molten mixture and baking it in furnaces.

As might be expected in the case of such uniquely skilled labor, the window-glass blowers organized a national union in 1865, and the other skilled glass workers followed in 1867. The window-glass manufacturers also formed an association. Shielded after 1861 by a very high protective tariff, and mostly congregated in eastern Ohio and western Pennsylvania, employers and workers were able to get along with backward technology, which used more labor and led to high costs. In 1900 the Chambers works at New Kensington, on the Allegheny River northeast of Pittsburgh, for example, said by local enthusiasts to be the most "thoroughly equipped in the world," were seen by a scholarly technical historian to be rather an illustration of the fact that American glassmaking was "substantially what it had been for centuries, an art and a handicraft." [1]

Widespread substitution of natural gas for coal as a source of heat had spread the glass industry to the Ohio oil area, but the shift in plants had been from the east rather than from the Pittsburgh area, whose primacy was undiminished in 1900. The change in fuel did not immediately bring the new European technology to companies producing window glass, where competition was well controlled. Tank furnaces instead of pots for

1. Pierce Davis, *The Development of the American Glass Industry* (Cambridge: Harvard University Press, 1949), pp. 181–182.

melting and the Lubbers cylinder blower, both available in the 1880s, were generally adopted only after 1900, and sheet drawing, the final step in near mechanization of window glass, was first used in America by the Libby, Owens Company in 1917.

The great development of textiles in both eastern and western Pennsylvania from early in the nineteenth century on was in part a result of the growth of the glass, iron, and machinery industries. These companies used chiefly male workers and left many wives and daughters available for work in carpet, sail, and cloth factories. In 1900 Pennsylvania led the nation in yardage of textile produced.

Tanning of leather and manufacture of leather goods had traditions of hand skills reaching back to the earliest days of the colony. Always a large cattle- and hog-raising area, the state had immense and readily accessible hemlock forests to supply the best bark for tanning. In contrast to glassmaking, where very great technical skill was needed in a few processes that controlled the whole final output, leather-working skills were diffused over the various operations and could be acquired reliably from normal apprenticeship. In such an industry, which involved tanned hides as well as shoes, saddles, bags, and gloves, there developed a built-in upward cycle: the large number of craftsmen led to continual small mechanical improvements in processes in which America was said to lead the world, and these machines, in turn, led to reduced costs and expansion of the available market. For all such mixtures of work by hand and machines, the large concentration of population in the river valleys around Philadelphia and Pittsburgh was a great stimulant. One should never forget the unusual degree of self-sufficiency in the industrialization of Pennsylvania.

But it is also true that in glass, leather, or even textiles, general economic development did not hinge upon this particular regional production. Imports could have substituted for any part of these without interfering with the more basic progress in steel, machinery, timber, agriculture, chemicals, and, later, in electricity. In both glass and leather Pennsylvania enjoyed what economists call a "comparative advantage" by having the needed raw materials in abundance. For textiles there was abundant female labor. Each such industry might have flourished without tariff protection from imports, and each produced its share of the growing national product, but they were not indispensable to industrial greatness.

Coal and iron were dramatically different. The nations that developed these resources in the mid-nineteenth century came to rule the world, and their citizens to enjoy previously unknown standards of living. The abundance of these sinews of industrialism all over Pennsylvania, however, led also to the discovery of other valuable but less essential minerals.

In the mid-century development of non-ferrous metals, Philadelphian Joseph Wharton was outstanding. A member of an old and wealthy family, he was educated by special tutors and by his own subsequent reading and experience in chemistry, geology, mineralogy, and metallurgy. In one of his early ventures he helped found and, for some three years (1853–1856), managed the Lehigh Zinc Company. In 1857 he was one of the founders of the Saucon, later the Bethlehem Iron Company. When he retired from the presidency of the company in 1904, it had become Bethlehem Iron and Steel, and was second only to United States Steel within the industry. Meanwhile, finding an abandoned nickel mine at Gap, where travelers came through the Chester County hills into the broad Lancaster plain, this imaginative metallurgist built a processing plant in Camden that turned out nickel and copper alloys. In 1875, he produced pure metallic nickel for the first time in America; this achievement reorganized the minting of fractional currency for the nation.

But iron and steel were to prove so vital that the achievements of Wharton and others in that field dwarfed other metallurgical advances. The fifties were years of portent rather than of abrupt change in the iron industry. The great railroad boom from 1850 to 1854 revived the demand for rails, and with the help of tariff protection encouraged a large expansion in domestic production. Cambria Iron Works at Johnstown did particularly well after the plant superintendent John Fritz introduced the three-high rolling mill, which economized on both labor and heat by allowing hot rails, or sheets, to be passed alternately through the rollers in both directions without removal. Some credit for adopting the innovation, not regarded as useful in England, should also go to General Manager Daniel J. Morrell of Cambria, who was one of the historic leaders of the iron and steel industry.

Attempts at making crucible, or blister, steel continued on a small scale in both the eastern and western parts of the state, but the German or Swedish immigrants who directed the processes relied on experience rather than on chemical understanding of what they were doing. Consequently, good runs that were fit for making edged tools alternated with poor ones, and imported steel was more reliable for this purpose.

The great American innovator in the transition from iron to mass-produced steel was William Kelly. Kelly was originally from Pittsburgh, but after his marriage to a Kentucky girl, he set up a small iron works near Eddysville, Kentucky. Just as Henry Bessemer had done in England, Kelly accidentally discovered that unheated air blown through iron rich in carbon heated the metal still more by burning up the excess carbon. This not only eliminated the need for charcoal in the forging furnace but produced steel (iron with less than two percent carbon) as an end product.

Bessemer in England and Kelly in Kentucky suffered equally from lack of fundamental chemical knowledge. They didn't really understand what they were doing and consequently couldn't produce uniform results. A blast applied too strongly or for too long would eliminate practically all carbon and oxidize the iron leaving a crumbly, useless mass. In England the problem of control was solved by Robert Mushet who, through chemical experimentation, found that adding spiegeleisen, a common mixed ore (plentiful in Pennsylvania), would both control excess oxygen and insure a desirable amount of carbon. What was happening was practically complete elimination of the original carbon in the iron and controlled recarbonization from the spiegeleisen. If the original ore contained large amounts of phosphorus, however, which nearly all the ore in the Pennsylvania river valleys did, the Mushet process would not produce a steel with the desired hardness combined with flexibility.

William Kelly in far-off Eddysville didn't read British scientific or engineering journals, and only later did he know of Bessemer's and Mushet's discoveries. Working with small converters in the woods back of his main plant from 1851 on, Kelly produced enough acceptable steel to submit, with a written description of the cold-blast process, for a U.S. patent, which he obtained in 1857, over the protests of the Bessemer representatives. Then came the panic of that year, the bankruptcy of Kelly's iron business, and sale of the new patent to his father-in-law for $1,000. Daniel Morrell, at Cambria, displaying his usual business and managerial insight, had some of his partners join him in acquiring the patent and hiring Kelly. Told to go on experimenting, Kelly "invented" a tiltable converter and worked with it, producing some bad batches and some good. He learned that too strong a blast was not as good as more air at lower pressure, and presumably he used Mushet's spiegeleisen but never learned about the proper qualities in ores. In 1862 he gave up further work at Johnstown and returned to Kentucky to manufacture axes.

Noting the variations in Kelly's results, Morrell, in 1860, hired a chemist, Captain Robert J. Hunt, who was probably the first professional scientist in an American iron works. Thus by the early sixties the process for steel making was fairly well understood chemically, but its commercial use was still questionable, chiefly because suitable pig iron was hard to find. Only time would tell whether steel rails, destined to be the early massive use for steel, wore better than wrought-iron rails, and obviously the phosphoric ores of eastern Pennsylvania and northern New Jersey were poor for either the Bessemer or Kelly process of steel making.

Lake Superior ores had reached ironmasters at Pittsburgh in the early 1850s, and the general impression was that they were nearly pure. Consequently Daniel Morrell, James Park, Jr., and E. B. Ward, all Cambria stockholders, working with Z. S. Durfee in a plant at Wyandotte, Michigan, in which Ward had an interest, tried making steel from the up-state ore. The process worked smoothly, but the cost of fuel made the location commercially a poor one, and no one realized how much success had depended on Lake Superior ore. Since none of the Michigan customers wanted the steel (it was finally sent to Chicago for rolling) the sensible plan seemed to be to build a plant nearer to both coal and markets. Meanwhile, Alexander L. Holley, working with mill owners at Troy, N.Y., using Lake Champlain ores, had found that the types of impurity in those ores made success with the Bessemer and Mushet process unlikely.

The inventions and practical knowledge necessary for making steel were now fairly complete, and the problem was to find proper ores for rail and other types of production in the United States. In this phase the great figure was Holley. A man devoted to engineering and structural design, he had some of the background and versatility of a Nicholas Biddle. Born near Lakeville, Connecticut, where his father was a large manufacturer of cutlery, in 1853 he earned one of the earliest degrees given in science at Brown University. While he had a fair background in chemistry and physics, his true enthusiasm was drawing plans for machines. As a freshman in college he had published an article in the *American Research Journal* and two years later invented an automatic cut-off for steam engines. Like so many of the bright boys of his generation, he was fascinated by locomotives, just as Biddle, living through the formation of new governments, had been absorbed in political economy. And like Biddle he loved to write. For nearly twenty years, while he was designing the great steel plants of the nation, he was a correspondent for the *New York Times,* to which he contributed nearly three hundred articles, and as hobbies he wrote fiction and poetry. In 1860, at age 28, he wrote *American and European Railroad Practice,* which led, two years later, to a trip to Europe to study munitions making for the Union government and railroad operations for a group of company presidents. Seeing the Bessemer process in operation, he arranged with two New York backers to buy the rights for use in the United States. After a year's training in Bessemer's works, Holley designed the pilot plant at Troy for the first attempt to use the process in America.

His results at the Winslow and Griswold company in Troy and the experiences at Wyandotte demonstrated that most eastern ore had too much phosphorus (over 4 percent); that cheap fuel made Pennsylvania the best location for production; and that the well-tested Bessemer method seemed more reliable than the Kelly process. The handsome and gracious Holley was no doubt a major influence in bringing the New Yorkers and Pennsylvanians together in pooling the two patents. The Cambria group with its Kelly patent was allotted a three-tenths share in the pool, while seven-tenths went to Holley, John F. Winslow, and John A. Griswold, of New York, the holders of the American Bessemer rights. To make the pool secure, the Patent Office was persuaded in 1866 to recognize the Bessemer patent. It should be noted that, compared to the profits of successful steel companies, the payments asked for patent rights were almost negligible. The patent holders joined in organizing the Pennsylvania Steel Company, in which J. Edgar Thomson, president of the Pennsylvania Railroad, and other Philadelphia users of steel bought stock. Supervised by Holley, the new company built a plant in 1867 at Steelton on the Susquehanna, a little below Harrisburg.

Neither this company nor Andrew Carnegie's simultaneously organized Freedom Iron and Steel Company had immediate success. Both learned the need for reliable sources of pig, preferably within the control of the company, but not until 1868 was it chemically demonstrated that ore either from the Lake Superior region or from abroad was the best. Neither type of ore, however, was inexpensive or easy to secure in large quantities at this time. While the Pennsylvania Company, practically owned by its best customers, made a substantial success of producing steel, Carnegie temporarily decided that because of the shortage of good pig for Bessemer, the business was not worth the troubles involved with new processes and skeptical buyers. Until 1873 he remained an ardent preacher of the virtues of iron rails rather than steel.

The advancing technology of steel making during the first generation of American production continued to owe much to Holley. His chief improvements on British practice were placing the converters above floor level so their quickly worn bottoms could be replaced by machines, arranging them so that at least two could be serviced by a single mechanized ladle crane, and conveying the poured ingots away by rail. In 1875 Holley estimated the American converters made three batches, or blows, of steel per day compared to one for the British. Hence three dozen converters in the United States produced as much steel as one hundred in the United Kingdom.

Other developments beside the introduction of Bessemer that occurred during this generation were to be important for the longer-run future of the industry. William and Friedrich Siemans of Germany perfected a regenerative furnace greatly superior to the reverberatory type in use, and as it had not been patented by an American representative, it was copied by James Pratt, Jr., of Pittsburgh in 1867. The Siemans furnace was particularly valuable for open-hearth steel. Abram S. Hewitt acquired the United States rights to the somewhat similar Martin brothers furnace, patented in France. While unsuccessful at his own Trenton works, he made good returns from selling the rights.

The next great development after Kelly and Bessemer, was open-hearth steel, really an extension of the puddling process for iron. Pig iron and scrap were placed in an open, saucerlike receptacle, and heated to the high temperatures made possible by the Siemans furnace. Reduction of the percentage of carbon was easier to test and supervise than in the closed Bessemer converters, and hence purer steel could, in theory, be consistently produced. Shortly after Hewitt's failure with the open-hearth process at Trenton, William Butcher, from England, tried it unsuccessfully in a Philadelphia steel works financed by iron wholesaler Philip S. Justice. In 1871 the bankrupt works were acquired by the widely known Philadelphia machine-tool maker William Sellers, who organized the Midvale Steel Company in that city. The major problem had been the same as that of the Bessemer process, finding suitable pig. The men who solved the problem were William F. Durfee, who had supervised the Wyandotte Bessemer experiment for his brother Z. S. Durfee, and Charles F. Brinley, a postgraduate student of metallurgy from Yale. They studied the ores, tabulated the results of trial runs, redesigned machinery, and made the process successful. Since it was most efficient with small converters, open-hearth was well suited for high-grade special steels, but more expensive for mass production of rails. Midvale open-hearth, for example, was used for making parts of the famous Eads Bridge over the Mississippi at St. Louis, but not for the bulk of the structure.

Nothing could take the place of chemical knowledge of ore, but understanding these characteristics still left the problem of reducing the ore's unwanted ingredients. Sidney Gilchrist Thomas, a London police-court clerk who built a miniature Bessemer converter in a home laboratory, experimented tirelessly with methods of separating phosphorus from iron. His first basic discovery was that at temperatures above 2500° F. the phosphorus would combine with lime and could be skimmed off as slag. The second step was to find a furnace lining that would stand such temperatures, and this was his patented (1877) "basic" liner of dolomite brick. Thomas's cousin Percy C. Gilchrist, a chemist in a steel company, tried the process on a larger scale and found that it worked. As usual the steel men were hard to convince. Carnegie acquired the patent for use by the Bessemer Steel Association, and after much negotiation over licensing arrangements, the patent was made generally available in the United States in 1881.

The Thomas basic liner was not a cure-all for phosphorus. The reduction was sufficient for open-hearth, but not always for Bessemer. Since steelmasters also preferred the greater control possible with open-hearth, it slowly gained on the Bessemer process until it surpassed it in volume of production after 1900. But during the period up to the 1880s, Bessemer, made increasingly from the pure Lake Superior ores, was the important American steel. Pennsylvania Steel, starting in 1867, Jones and Laughlin about 1870, Cambria in 1871, Bethlehem in 1872, and Carnegie, McCandless in 1875, together with the Scranton Steel Company and works at Joliet, Illinois, became the major producers.

In 1864, before the advent of Bessemer, an American Iron and Steel Association was formed primarily to assemble information and lobby for higher tariffs. Two years later an American Iron Masters Laboratory was jointly sponsored in Philadelphia, but in organizing the new steel industry, neither was as important as agreements among the inner circle of the big companies.

By 1875, when Carnegie's Edgar Thomson works came into production, there were still few enough major competitors and customers to make co-operation seem possible. Meeting in Philadelphia, company leaders formed the Bessemer Steel Association to allocate production quotas. The men whom Carnegie called the "Fathers in Israel" because they controlled the industry, officers from the leading American steel companies were all present: Samuel Felton of Pennsylvania Steel, E. Y. Townshend and Daniel Morrell of Cambria, Joseph Wharton of Bethlehem, William Scranton of Scranton Iron and Steel, Benjamin F. Jones of Jones and Laughlin, and the newcomer Andrew Carnegie. Carnegie, with the most modern works from Holley's latest design, had the whip hand in threats of price warfare and emerged with a top quota equaled only by Cambria. From this time on, as with other pools, periods of price warfare in slack times alternated with adherence to prices and quotas when demand exceeded supply, but always the relatively few big steel companies kept close watch on each other, in both co-operation and competition.

Holley had been the American architect of steel technology. Andrew Carnegie was a leader in demonstrating tactics for competitive success in large-scale steel manufacturing and in timing the adoption of technological innovations. Even though the iron and steel industry might have developed approximately the same way had there been no Carnegie, historians would have known much less about both this industry and business practices in general, from 1860 to 1900. Coming from a family interested in public affairs and sure of his own long-run importance, he saved early letters and kept a diary; he made many speeches and wrote numerous articles. All of these activities were quite contrary to the secretive, nonliterate businessmen of the day. Furthermore, he ran his companies dictatorially and by remote control, so that detailed board minutes had to be sent to him and he wrote detailed replies. In contrast we know about Rockefeller chiefly from reminiscences dictated decades later, and about Gould,

Scott, Thomson, and Vanderbilt only from a few letters, saved by chance in railroad offices. As a result, historians have to see the great state and national development of steel through accounts biased by the words and actions of Carnegie.

He was conditioned by family upbringing for a radical or innovative role in business. The son of a small linen manufacturer in the politically advanced although ancient borough (city) of Dunfermline, northwest of Edinburgh, Scotland, where nearly half the population was in the linen trade, his earliest recollections were of talk about economics and politics. When he was growing up, his uncle and his great-uncle were active radical Whig politicians working for Parliamentary adoption of a new code of democratic rights known as the Charter. The young boy listened at home to some of the leading British liberals, and to endless family discussions of political and worldly philosophy. The Carnegies, as fitted their advanced political stand, were freethinkers, but Andrew's mother found much pleasure in the Puritan sermons of William Ellery Channing.

As master weavers of linen and damask increasingly felt the pressures of factory competition, Carnegie's father's business declined until by the late forties he was operating only his own loom, and to help the family finances Andrew's mother had opened a shop. She was the strong member of the household and instilled in her son both a desire for heroic achievement and a feeling for the superiority of people with ideas and energy over the common lot of men. Present-day psychologists speculate that a strong, supportive mother and a retiring father may produce great self-confidence in a child. At least it did in young Carnegie. When the Charter failed ignominiously in Parliament in 1848, and there seemed little chance of restoring the family's income in Dunfermline, the Carnegies migrated to join relatives in Pittsburgh.

Carnegie belongs to that group of immigrants from rigorous, advanced business environments who brought to the United States a sharpness in trading, a keen regard for costs, and an ability to manipulate people. Above all else, Carnegie was a supersalesman, a man who from his first advent as a proprietor took over the function of marketing as his special preserve. His major historic role was as an international marketer for certain products of expanding mass production, and there were few modern sales techniques on the wholesale level that he over-looked. As he moved into iron, he cultivated friendships with all the railroad presidents and their purchasing agents; when abroad he made sure he met the large buyers of steel in both business and government, and whenever possible he gave press interviews on the progress of America and the steel industry.

By the time the 24-year-old adolescent prodigy had become superintendent of the Western Division of the Pennsylvania, railroads were the chief customers of the iron industry. At this time it was not considered unethical for railroad managers to own stock or silent partnerships in firms supplying the road, and most fortunes in railroading came from such "side shows," par-ticularly those in coal, iron, and land. Certainly few energetic and ambitious railroad managers of the time were not active in such allied investments.

A usual procedure was for men organizing railroad supply companies to give the proper officers of the chief customers shares of stock, which could be paid for from subsequent divi-dends. Always on the watch for business opportunities, Car-negie, having at this time neither wife nor children to support, was able to amass an unusual amount of personal capital in oil lands, iron works, sleeping-car and bridge-construction compa-nies before he was thirty. In 1863, while still a moderate-salaried railroad manager, he had an income of $40,000 a year. Since he shared many of his opportunities with Vice-President Tom Scott, in whose office he had originally worked, and with President Thomson, he became a kind of informal partner in managing the group's investments, a business that proved so profitable and time-consuming that in 1865 he resigned from the railroad.

Two years earlier Carnegie had joined other Pennsylvania Railroad managers in forming the Piper and Shiffler Company for constructing iron bridges. With iron rapidly superseding wood for bridges all over the nation, Carnegie decided that for a man with railroad connections this was one of the best business opportunities. In 1865 the company expanded to include the engineer responsible for bridges on the Pennsylvania, and Tom Scott, who held his stock in Carnegie's name; the firm was renamed the Keystone Bridge Company.

Concentrating on the marketing of bridges led Carnegie inevitably into a network of financial interrelations, illustrative of much business practice both then and now. First he would participate in a construction corporation to finance the building of the bridge, and as a director of the bridge manufacturing company, he voted a building contract to his construction company. Then representing both firms, he needed to make sure that railroads intending to use the bridge were going to be financially able to reach it or, if the roads were already constructed, to be able to pay for a new iron structure. Money, or its equivalent, to cover building costs could come from the construction company accepting as partial payment bonds (at bargain prices) in both the railroads and the bridge company and then getting cash from selling the first-mortgage bonds of either company to the public. Since the Pennsylvania Railroad group had an excellent reputation in Europe, Carnegie found it expedient to become an informal international investment banker, selling bridge and railroad bonds on commission. In this he was joining many other Americans interested in railroads who took trips to England or Europe to persuade Baring Brothers, Junius S. Morgan, the Hopes, or other Continental houses to take portions of new issues.

To conduct this business Carnegie moved to a hotel suite in New York, opened an office there on Broad Street in 1867, and was never again a resident of Pennsylvania, although his investments were increasingly confined to companies in this state. By late 1872 the railroad boom had saturated the British market with American stocks and bonds, and Carnegie saw little future in such marketing. He warned Scott and Thomson to get out of uncompleted western railroads, but neither man followed his advice.

Having seen the success of Jones and Laughlin, Cambria, and Bethlehem in turning out Bessemer steel, and the railroads' preference for it, Carnegie decided to sell many of his other securities and build a large steel works. This decision exemplified the good luck that seemed to hover over him, but it was also an indication of his keen sensitivity to business trends. Although he didn't predict the panic of 1873, he did sense the dangers in the oversold foreign security markets.

While Carnegie was spending most of his time in Europe and New York, his only brother, Thomas, was looking after affairs in Pennsylvania. As conservative and retiring as Andrew was bold and aggressive, Tom made an ideal advisor, to whom his impetuous older brother reluctantly listened. They never seem to have had a serious disagreement while Tom, the meticulous accountant and examiner of detail, kept some restraint on Andrew's ever-soaring ambitions.

Tom Carnegie had first entered the iron business in 1861 as a silent partner, along with Thomas Miller, purchasing agent of the Pittsburgh, Fort Wayne and Chicago Railroad, in the Freedom Iron Company. Two years later, when Miller was having difficulties in another iron company with his partners the Kloman brothers, he appealed to Andrew to make peace. As with the proverbial camel in the tent, the settlement ended with Tom Carnegie in the company and Anthony Kloman outside. The new firm was composed of Tom Carnegie, Miller, Andrew Kloman, and Henry Phipps, Jr. Its main product was iron for bridges. The following year, in order to appease Miller, who had received bad treatment from Kloman and Phipps, Andrew Carnegie joined with him in the Cyclops Iron Company. Thus Andrew gained experience with the problems of three iron companies. In the course of disagreements among this group of partners, Andrew Carnegie demonstrated his belief that a keen, cold eye for opportunity was a far more valuable business asset than any particular ethical principle. His practices, in contrast to his writings, suggest that he proceeded on the belief that progress justified its moral costs, and that in business as in war there could be no fixed rules. In these attitudes he probably differed little from other outwardly sanctimonious financiers such as those among the famed Boston Brahmins.

Carnegie had begun to build the J. Edgar Thomson Bessemer works at Braddock on the Monongahela before the panic of 1873 threw the business world into confusion, but because of his earlier decision to sell his stocks, he was able to complete the plant in 1875 at depression prices for construction, with only some relatively small loans. Three things insured his success: the continuing demand for steel rails, the fact that his was the latest plant designed and supervised by Alexander Holley, and Daniel Morrell's unwise employee policies at Cambria, its chief competitor.

Morrell believed in paying the lowest possible wages; consequently he cut them during the depression. George Fritz, the able plant superintendent who, together with his brother John, then with Wharton at Bethlehem, had built up Cambria, believed high wages increased productivity. His chief assistant, Captain William R. Jones, thought the same way. As a result, when Fritz retired, Morrell refused to promote Jones, who resigned. Holley had no trouble selling Jones to Carnegie, and in all, the new JET plant recruited some two-hundred discontented Cambria workers. Thus Carnegie, whose knowledge of iron and steel was purely theoretical, acquired by sheer good fortune one of the most innovative and popular plant managers in history.

Actually, between 1870 and 1890 there were no great innovations in the acid (silicon brick furnace lining) Bessemer process. The biggest improvements were in blast-furnace output and fuel consumption. In 1870 a single furnace was expected to produce fifty tons of iron per day and burn up double that tonnage in coal. By 1890 furnaces were regularly producing over ten times as much iron while using only about five times as much coke. The improvements had come gradually from better furnace design, more efficient use of heat, and particularly from faster, mechanized handling of materials. Although not as celebrated as Bessemer or Thomas, Jones made inventions in all of these operations and kept the Carnegie works among the leaders. For example, just before he was killed by an explosion in 1889, he invented a mixing machine that received the iron from several furnaces and turned out a uniform pig for the Bessemer converters.

The spur to fundamental change in the industry was a temporary shortage of Lake Superior ore in the early 1880s as the northern Michigan mines became exhausted. This encouraged experiments with the Thomas process of basic open-hearth production, which could use the still plentiful Pennsylvania ores. The historic Cornwall Furnace, near Harrisburg, for example, reached new peaks of production in the eighties. With increased experience, steel men came to prefer the open-hearth process.

In addition to the Thomas basic furnace lining, which allowed the use of local resources, imported ore from many areas helped to keep the eastern steel industry prosperous. By the end of the century the Port of Philadelphia received ore from nations bordering the Black Sea, Brazil, British India, Cuba, the island of Elba, Spain, and Sweden, each valued for different qualities. Smaller eastern companies concentrated on specialties such as seamless tubing. Ellwood Ivins of Philadelphia is credited with drawing the first American cold-rolled tubes around 1890. The tube business flourished from the demand of bicycle companies, and in 1899 Summerill Tubing was started at Bridgeport on the Schuylkill by S. L. Gable.

Large companies made both specialties and heavy structural parts. Bethlehem near the Delaware, rolled the first armor plate in 1890 and was soon followed by the Carnegie works. Next to Carnegie's Keystone Company near Pittsburgh, the Pencoyd Company just up the Schuylkill from Philadelphia made the largest volume of structural parts for bridges. Of all the eastern mills, Midvale, within the city of Philadelphia, had the widest variety of finished products, including wire, springs, and guns. It also benefited from new ideas for alloys, and for organizational efficiencies introduced between 1878 and 1884 by its young plant manager Frederick W. Taylor.

Few Pennsylvanians have received the western-world attention given to Frederick W. Taylor. The son of a Germantown lawyer, Taylor refused to enter Harvard Law School because of poor eyesight and instead went into factory work. In 1878 he joined Midvale as a common laborer. Apparently gaining some improvement in his sight, he took a mechanical-engineering degree from Stevens Institute in 1883, through evening work, and became Midvale's chief engineer. In 1893 he retired from salaried activity and opened a Philadelphia office to provide advice on systematizing shop management and manufacturing costs. While advising at Bethlehem Steel, he met J. Maunsel

White, who co-operated with him in perfecting through heat processes a high-speed tool steel with a cutting capacity 200 to 300 percent higher than the regular product. But Taylor's greatest claim to fame was as the publicizer of a system of plant organization that he called scientific management. His ideas of time-motion study of job operations, of foremen specialized in certain tasks, and of rewarding high productivity by "piece rates," struck a responsive chord in the managers of many factories in America and Europe. He summarized his mature system in *Scientific Management* published in 1911. By then he had helped to build a whole new profession of industrial engineering.

Meanwhile important changes were taking place in the structure of the Pennsylvania steel industry. The continuing need for cheaper, relatively pure ores was satisfied only by the discovery of new deposits in the region around the west end of Lake Superior. Ironically, the Lake Vermillion mines that began the great extension to the north and west came from the explorations of an expedition financed by Philadelphians Charlemagne Tower and R. H. Lee. In a dozen years of initial development, however, the most important figures were John D. Rockefeller as an absentee owner of mines and railroads and Henry W. Oliver of Pittsburgh as the most active organizer of production. The latter, whose father had been a saddlery maker in downtown Pittsburgh, had become important as an iron and steel manufacturer and local railroad promoter. From 1870 to 1892 he was influential in bringing both the Baltimore and Ohio and the Pittsburgh and Lake Erie to the city, thus breaking the monopoly of the Pennsylvania Railroad. In these activities he had the tacit support of Carnegie (who had known him as a telegraph messenger boy) of John D. Rockefeller, and of the Vanderbilts, all of whom he had aided in contests with the Pennsylvania Railroad. Ultimately the Vanderbilt lines annexed the Pittsburgh and Lake Erie.

As Oliver formed his Oliver Iron Mining Company and moved into the new ore fields in 1892, he was long on influential friends and short on money. Like so many American entrepreneurs, he was always expanding in too many directions, and his iron and steel company was soon in financial trouble. Hence when he had assured himself first of the value of the "soft" Mesabi ore and later of the "hard" Gogebic, he had to turn to Frick and Carnegie for cash. Frick was always favorable, but Carnegie either from conservatism or super-shrewdness had to be dragged along step by step with options for stock purchases in Oliver's operations sometimes held up by Carnegie's control of the steel company until within a few days of their termination. Meanwhile, Oliver's operations in Pittsburgh had to wait for the necessary cable from Scotland. Not surprisingly, by the time Oliver had secured the most valuable rights, the Carnegie Steel Company owned five-sixths of Oliver Iron Mining.

With control of ore supplies more than sufficient for its own needs, the Carnegie Company insured cheap access by building its own ore boats and taking over the operation of a railroad from Pittsburgh to Conneaut on Lake Erie. This system, copied to some extent by other steel companies, led to a reduction in the price of American steel that made it competitive with that of Britain and Germany in world markets, thus largely increasing its potential area for sales.

The great expansion in steel from 1895 on brought internal troubles to Carnegie's business empire. Basically the difficulty was that he delegated full managerial responsibility to a few able men in Pittsburgh, but tried to exercise in absentia ultimate authority, even in quite small matters, from wherever he happened to be. Legally the company was a closely held corporation in which each officer was allotted shares of stock and was referred to as a "partner," but in which Carnegie's holding of over 58 percent was always decisive. Probably no company can be satisfactorily run in that way, but, at least, three factors made it impossible in the case of Carnegie Steel.

First, Carnegie, with his large share of the dividends and numerous outside investments, wanted to use the earnings of the steel company for vertical expansion of the company's operations rather than for dividends to the "partner" stockholders. The latter, often young men on modest salaries with families to bring up, wanted some distribution of the wealth that in the nineties was being accumulated by their company in the tens of millions annually. In fact, even the old "partners" such as Henry Phipps and George Lauder (Carnegie's cousin) wanted more dividends. This phase of the Carnegie troubles reminds one of the suit of the Dodge brothers against Henry Ford to force dividend payments a generation later.

A second endemic problem was that the Frick Coke Company, which produced most of the Connellsville coke, while controlled by Carnegie, had substantial minority stockholders who had no interest in the steel company. Thus there could be, and were, severe disputes about the intercompany price of coke.

That structural anomaly was enhanced by the third and ultimately the critical cause of internal trouble, the fact that Henry Clay Frick, who had built up the coke company as his own creation, became operating head of both companies and had a character fully as strong and more steadily determined than Carnegie's. With these elements interacting, perhaps the remarkable thing was that the personal relationships remained reasonably amiable for nearly twenty years before their final breakdown.

Next to Frick in managerial authority was an able technical man Charles M. Schwab. In 1897 he became president, while Frick remained chairman of the board, and Carnegie continued to dominate although holding no office. The three men offered striking contrasts in personality. Carnegie was imaginative, mercurial, and dictatorial; Schwab easy-going and genial, with a keen eye for economies based on new technology; while Frick was a strict and humorless administrator with a pride and a temper that Carnegie often failed to respect. In the works, however, all three agreed on rigid economy, close supervision, no relations with labor unions, and long working hours. Their major disagreement regarding policy, aside from that of Frick and Carnegie over coke prices, was that Carnegie wanted to use the large profits to integrate toward the making of the various finished steel products, such as wire, tubing, hoops, and cars, whereas both Frick and Schwab wanted to invest in new equipment to give them an impregnable position in billets, sheets, and other primary forms of steel.

By 1897 as profits soared to unexpected heights, Carnegie

began to give hints from Skibo Castle in Scotland or his villa on
the Riviera that he would be willing to retire from an active
interest in the company. This led to an effort by a Chicago-
based syndicate to buy the company for resale to the public, but
Carnegie disapproved of the syndicate leaders. Next an effort by
Carnegie to buy out Frick at the book value of his shares, as
provided for in an old agreement, was contested in the Pennsylvania courts. Alarmed that publicity regarding the company
could lead to charges that its great profits were due to high tariff
and thus might defeat the Republican party in the election of
1900, the contending factions were temporarily brought together
in a reorganized company capitalized at $320 million, of which
Frick had a $31 million share, but was not on the board.

Carnegie, while forced to recognize the real value of his
''partner's'' holdings, was still in control and ready for action.
His plan as of 1900 was to break the hold of the eastern trunklines, and particularly the Pennsylvania on steel rates, by joining with the Gould interests in new connections that would ultimately give Carnegie a major influence on all freight rates in
the ''trunkline territory.'' This possibility immediately aroused
J. Pierpont Morgan, who since the middle eighties had been
striving for a community of interest to bring harmony between
the trunklines. Morgan was then playing a large part in the
American phase of the movement—that was encouraged all over
the world from 1898 to around 1902—to merge competing business firms by the unprecedentedly easy marketing of new securities. Having already entered steel on a large scale by putting
together Illinois and Ohio properties, Morgan thought that addition of the Carnegie Company would give the combination effective control of the market for primary steel. Such action by
Morgan would also discourage Carnegie from moving further
into transportation and finished steel products.

In the flush times of 1901, Schwab rather easily engineered a
Morgan offer to Carnegie. On the proviso that Carnegie's and
Lauder's shares in the $1.4 billion holding company be paid for
in first mortgage gold bonds based on all the properties of the
combine, Carnegie accepted $226 million. Schwab continued

for three years as president of the new United States Steel Corporation. Many years later the Supreme Court ruled that the corporation's share of nearly half the primary market was not used to restrain trade. The ruling was probably correct, since the early history of the greatly overcapitalized company was not one of unusual profitability.

From the standpoint of Pennsylvania's unique position in the nation of the nineteenth century, the history of the Carnegie companies and the formation of United States Steel is usually overemphasized as a symbol of change. This company, originally a Pennsylvania enterprise from all standpoints, ore, works, and control, although its head office remained in Pittsburgh, came to be controlled from the 1870s on by Carnegie, who lived in New York City; came to rely increasingly on ore from Minnesota; and finally came to be combined with plants in other states. But the other steel companies mentioned here kept their main operations in Pennsylvania, and large firms in new industries arose within the state.

The rapid growth and lively business atmosphere of Pittsburgh, particularly, attracted young inventors looking for financial backing, and among them was George Westinghouse. The son of an agricultural-implement manufacturer of Schenectady, New York, he found it impossible to get sufficient local business backing for his inventions, so he came to Pittsburgh looking for financial support. Except for three months at Union College, Westinghouse lacked formal higher education, but he had served as an assistant engineer in the navy during the last part of the Civil War. As soon as he was mustered out, he started filing for and receiving patents, several hundred during his lifetime, most of them for useful improvements on existing processes. Attempting to market a better connecting frog for railroad switches brought him to Pittsburgh, but in the same year, 1869, he took out his most famous and basic patent, that for the railroad airbrake. After a successful demonstration on the Panhandle road in Pittsburgh, he received enough financial support from a handful of railroad managers, such as A. J. Cassatt and Robert Pitcairn of the Pennsylvania, to organize the

Westinghouse Airbrake Company. He insured his brake's continued position in the field by patenting twenty subsequent improvements.

A good marketer as well as inventor, Westinghouse started manufacturing in Paris in 1879. Within a decade passenger trains all over the world were using his invention. Brakes that could grip almost simultaneously on fifty cars of a freight train involved problems that he finally solved in 1888.

This attractive young giant in energy and imagination meanwhile was moving into new fields. With natural gas gaining as a fuel and source of light in the Pittsburgh area in the late seventies, Westinghouse brought in a well close to his house in Homewood. To market the product, he bought the unused special charter of a firm called the Philadelphia Company that was allowed to do nearly everything but banking, including distribution of oil or gas. As business expanded, he protected his market by thirty-eight patents on gas transmission.

Inventing devices for stepping pressure in gas lines up and down, while he was also promoting the Union Switch and Signal Company of Pittsburgh, led him, from 1882 on, into thought about new possibilities in varying voltage in electrical current. By 1885 he had decided that the future of controlled variations in energy lay with electricity. Organizing the Westinghouse Electric Company, he moved as a pioneer into this new field of business and technology. From the start he saw the great potential advantages of alternating current, and bought the rights to the English Gaulard and Gibbs single-phase system. Soon his own engineers were improving all uses of alternating current. The William Stanley shell-type transformer, for example, developed in the Pittsburgh plant had many commercial advantages over the European models. Another member of the staff, Oliver B. Shallenberg, invented a meter that would register the consumption of electrical energy. Westinghouse hired Nikola Tesla, inventor of an alternating-current motor, and bought his United States patent. Late in 1886 hundreds of bulbs were lit by alternating current in Pittsburgh's suburb of Lawrenceville, four miles from the generating plant; this was the longest transmission of electricity in the United States at that time.

As in the case of Carnegie, these developments brought Westinghouse into conflict with the nation's large financial interests. A syndicate led by J. Pierpont Morgan had financed the Edison Electric Company, which supplied lights, by 1882, to downtown New York using direct current. For nearly a decade Thomas A. Edison led the direct-current interests in an attack on the dangers of alternating current, which could be transmitted at very high voltages on small wires. Political influence, for example, was used to have New York State execute criminals in electric chairs with alternating current. But the advantages of the latter, especially for long-distance transmission, were so great that ultimately Edison and Morgan organized General Electric Company, made peace with Westinghouse and his company, and in 1895 the two firms agreed on a pooling of patents. In this same year the great Niagara Falls Power Company, constructed by Westinghouse, commenced large production of alternating hydroelectric current.

Success continually inspired Westinghouse to invest more money in research, patents, and manufacturing facilities. In 1889 he started the company town of Wilmerding on Turtle Creek in East Pittsburgh, and gradually moved his main plants there. He also established many subsidiaries in England and on the Continent. By 1890 he was in financial difficulties that required reorganization of the company by the banking house of August Belmont. Once again, encouraged by soaring electrical-equipment sales in the early twentieth century, he expanded too rapidly with borrowed funds, and the panic of 1907 forced the electrical company into receivership. Although restored to nominal control in 1908, he was irked by the restraints imposed by the banks and retired in 1911 to devote the remaining three years of his life to further inventions.

Whereas Westinghouse was the normal optimistic, energetic, outgoing American type of entrepreneur, gifted with an unusual analytical mind, his fellow-townsman Andrew W. Mellon was more like John D. Rockefeller. Mellon was the retiring, thoughtful, and conservative risk-taker, who deplored public appearances and gave his nearly undivided attention to the business aspects of his investments. His father, Thomas, retired as a judge of the court of common pleas of Allegheny County and opened a private banking house in 1869, the same year that Andrew entered the University of Pittsburgh. When Andrew left the university in 1873, he tried a year in the lumber business before joining the Bank of Thomas Mellon & Sons.

As bankers Andrew and his brother Robert B. kept a watch on all the varied business activities of Pittsburgh. When their investing became more family-centered and less involved with their bank, they changed the private firm to the Mellon National Bank of Pittsburgh. By the end of the century the brothers were important holders of stock in banking, trust, and bridge companies, Gulf Oil, Koppers, American Locomotive, Standard Steel Car, Worthington Pump, Crucible Steel, Pittsburgh Coal, and Pittsburgh Reduction Company.

The latter was to become the Mellons' most important industrial interest. In 1886 Charles M. Hall had patented an electrolytic process for recovering metallic aluminum from the bauxite ores found in Alabama and Georgia. Like Westinghouse, Hall came to Pittsburgh to seek financial backing and found it in a group that included the Mellons. Their Pittsburgh Reduction Company was initially a small venture with a plant located in the city between Thirty-Second and Thirty-Third streets. The chief use of aluminum, still priced at about $4 a pound, was in optical and dental work. The first big change came in 1890 with the discovery of the value of aluminum for kitchen utensils. The next year the plant was moved to New Kensington, and an increased scale of production dropped the price to under 75c a pound. The rise of the automobile industry, in which aluminum was used both as a valuable steel alloy and for lightweight parts, and the greater use of electricity, which aluminum conducted well, was to create a mass demand for the new metal. But as late as 1903 production was less than 4,000 tons. Meanwhile, the company had established plants near Niagara Falls and in the Tennessee Valley, to be near hydroelectric power, and had begun an ore-cleaning operation in St. Louis. The greatest single upswing in demand for aluminum came from aircraft and other military purposes in World War I. Peacetime increase in the use of aircraft and more use in automobiles maintained a high level of production in the 1920s.

These two examples of major corporations that maintained their central control in Pittsburgh ran counter to the trends in national big business. The "great merger movement" of the turn of the century made large companies increasingly national in scope. Operations were moved to the most economic locations and frequently controlled from head offices near Wall Street. The Philadelphia and Pittsburgh metropolitan areas did not decline either financially or as manufacturing centers, but local companies were increasingly parts of national corporations and their local finance secondary to that arranged in New York City. Put still differently, a strongly local history of Pennsylvania's economic growth may be written up through the nineteenth century, from then on, economic development in the state has to be seen more as a reflection of national trends.

9

Early Industrial Society

*C*HANGING ways of doing business, new processes of manufacture, faster transportation, and flows of information, all combined in larger cities, brought pressures for change in practically every traditional way of living. Readjustments within the home and family in diets or living habits were gradual and in some cases unrealized by the people involved. Others like the coming of railroads and big central city office buildings remade the physical structure and appearance of society. One of the most obvious changes was the increasing concentration of people in urban centers. Population of the state's twenty largest cities was 782,000 in 1860—27 percent of the state's population. In 1910 these twenty cities totaled 4,236,000, or 55 percent. Before the Civil War only about a quarter of the people lived in the twenty cities, and except for Philadelphia, Pittsburgh, Reading, Lancaster, and Harrisburg, these "big" cities had under 10,000 inhabitants. In 1910, over half the people lived in cities with populations of 30,000 or more.

New forces drew people together in these increasingly crowded centers. Business establishments of all kinds found it necessary to be near railroad stations and preferably to have a choice of competing lines over which to receive or send shipments. Large plants needed railroad sidings and clustered close to the tracks. A choice of competing banks nearby was also important. The supply of labor in a city had a spiral effect on both growth and overcrowding. Workers looking for jobs came to towns where businesses were starting or expanding, and the larger the supply of various types of labor the more attractive the area was for new enterprise.

Another cause of the closely built up city was the need for workers to walk to their jobs. Horsecars were available in a few large centers from the middle 1850s on, and electric trolleys by the late 1880s, but a ride on either one cost too much for the low-paid worker. A man or woman averaging $1.00 to $1.25 a day hesitated to spend 10 cents getting to and from work. As a result, a firm needing a considerable number of employees either chose a location near a thickly built up part of the city, or formed a development company to build homes for workers.

In a laissez-faire system urban housing for workers seemed bound to become substandard. Construction workers were locally unionized in many areas where other workers were not and consequently were able to command wages much above the average. In addition, the failure of machine technology to make significant advances in home building created a continual need for expensive hand labor. Even if landlords took little profit, it was hard for a poorly paid, unskilled mine or plant worker to rent the product of skilled and highly paid hand labor. A small three-room row house with inside plumbing—providing city water and sewerage were available—might be afforded by a man and wife who both had low-paying jobs. But if they started raising a family, and as a result the wife's working hours were reduced, they couldn't meet the weekly rent. The usual recourse was to live with the growing family in two of the rooms and sublet the third one to lodgers, perhaps to several men working on different shifts.

Building construction was the principal type of new capital investment, and, except for farming, the building trades were the largest single type of employment. But because of seasonal layoffs, necessitated by four or five months of winter, even the high daily wages of these workers did not provide substantial annual incomes. In all the industrial nations the late nineteenth century was a period of low wages.

Looking at the urban housing problem in long perspective,

any real change required major innovations in government assistance, financial practices, or the organization of the construction industry. Surveys have indicated that in the relatively affluent mid-twentieth century, with high wages and low formation of capital, the average family is a net debtor until the head of the household reaches about age 35. Today the debt is carried by devices such as packaged mortgages, long-term instalment purchasing (essentially living from future wages), government subsidized housing, welfare payments, and unemployment insurance. None of these were available to the worker of the nineteenth or early twentieth century. Consequently as young workers' families grew in size, their standard of living tended to decline and their home surroundings to deteriorate, leading to unsanitary, ramshackle slums even in cities of only a few thousand people.

A minority of workers in construction, metals, railroading, woodworking, brewing, and glassmaking, who possessed special skills, a reputation for conscientious work, and frugal tastes, could be exceptions to the generally dismal picture. By manipulation of short-term second mortgages or through building and loan associations they might become the owners of small homes. Whether good sanitary conditions could be secured depended on local government. In general, central urban water systems came in the mid-nineteenth century and sewers only in 1880s and 1890s. A prominent historian has called the laggards the "risk-taking cities"; they risked poor health, disease, and epidemics rather than spend the money necessary for sanitation. Perhaps, however, the city fathers had little choice. Under the prevailing philosophy community leaders saw no reason why they should be taxed for other people's welfare or assume responsibility for the urban problems created by the growth of business.

Added to the general unpleasantness of the mine and mill cities, particularly in the western part of the state, was the pall of smoke that came from burning soft coal in homes and plants. Some saving features in Pennsylvania were the fact that in 1900 only seven cities had 50,000 or more inhabitants, that the eastern ones used anthracite, and that on most days in small cities smoke was dissipated over the surrounding open country.

Cheap housing was also increasingly overcrowded from the masses of immigrants who came to Pennsylvania between 1845 and 1914, more than to any state except New York. During the entire period the foreign-born averaged 15 to 16 percent of the population of the commonwealth. Initial immigrants were chiefly single men of working age who arrived in Philadelphia or the interior cities by rail from New York looking for whatever was offered in the way of immediate jobs. Sometimes they came to a Pennsylvania city under work contracts negotiated with agents before their boats docked in New York, or (from 1864 to 1885) under contracts negotiated abroad. In spite of widespread protest by native workers against such contracting for labor, it was never a very large business in the east. Few companies wanted to take a chance on paying for unskilled workers who might decide to disappear before working out their travel costs. Highly skilled workers who contracted on a personal and voluntary basis while still abroad were generally reliable and anxious to fulfill their agreement. Many companies used the temporary services of such Europeans to introduce or improve new processes. By putting some of his high American wages in a bank, the European could return home and improve his status, and perhaps about one third did so.

Immigrants spread all over the state strengthening and broadening the multicultural quality of the society. For example, Warren, a county seat way up in the northwest and a community growing rather slowly, nevertheless had, in 1870, 35 percent foreign-born workers. Among Warren's manual laborers the figure was 45 percent, of which there were 41 individuals from Ireland, 39 from France, 31 from Germany, 16 from England, 13 from Denmark, and 21 from a number of other nations. Among white-collar workers the foreign-born comprised only 20 percent, with the Germans and French the most numerous.[1]

These figures, of course, reflect the national origins of immigrants coming before 1890, but in the final great waves of immigration that ended in 1914, Pennsylvania also received

---

1. Michael P. Weber, "Occupational Mobility of Ethnic Minorities in Nineteenth Century Warren, Pennsylvania," in John E. Bodnar, ed., *The Ethnic Experience in Pennsylvania* (Lewisburg, Pa.: Bucknell University Press, 1973), p. 148.

large numbers from Italy and eastern Europe. Ruthenians from Austria-Hungary and Poles and other nationalities subject to Russia provided labor for the great expansion of coal mining in both the anthracite and bituminous fields. Members of these and other nationalities came primarily from rural areas in Europe, but by 1880 there was very little opportunity for new jobs in Pennsylvania agriculture. The decline in opportunity was due both to mechanization and to western competition in grain and meat. Except for some newcomers, particularly Italians, who rented small truck farms near the larger cities, the migrants went into mining, heavy industry, and numerous urban trades.

Unlike Boston or New York, neither Pittsburgh nor Philadelphia became immigrant cities. Philadelphia reached its highest percentage of foreign-born in the early 1870s at around 25 percent, and then gradually became increasingly native. Influencing the trend was replacement by their American-born children of the Irish immigrants who had come in such large numbers up through the middle of the century.

The chief newcomers to Philadelphia toward the end of the century were Italians and east European Jews. Some Italians spread across the state as construction workers, supplied to distant jobs by the padroni system of labor contracting, while many settled just south of central city in Philadelphia, from whence they could be taken by padronis in vans to wherever construction work was under way. A minority of Italians were in trade, but both workers and lower middle class clung to their Italian culture, community life, and the hope of returning to Italy. Only about one third of all Italian immigrants became permanent residents. Depending largely for jobs on city construction, Italian workers necessarily became loyal supporters of the local political bosses.

In contrast, the newly arrived Jews found work chiefly in textile finishing and garment making, which were done in small shops near the center of cities. But while most Jews came as unskilled workers, they intended to stay in the United States and to get ahead in American society. As a result they sent their children to high school and to college if possible, and eagerly seized upon chances for advancement in trades or professions.

Thus they gradually spread through cities and suburbs, leaving the stable Italian communities—in spite of shifting population—dominant in South Philadelphia and in similarly concentrated areas in other Pennsylvania cities.

Agriculture, largely carried on by people of the older immigrant stocks, such as German, Welsh, and Scotch-Irish, had had its ups and downs in Pennsylvania. The rapid expansion of the late eighteenth century, which had resulted in partial soil exhaustion in the southeast from overcropping, was followed after 1820 by revitalization from gypsum and lime fertilizer as well as crop rotation. In 1840 the state was still the nation's largest producer of wheat. During the forties and fifties Chester and Lancaster counties and parts of northern Delaware were the most progressive farm areas of the United States. As we have seen, plows and seed drills made near Philadelphia increased yields, first of corn and then of wheat; and new harrows, mowers, and harvesters pulled by horses rather than oxen joined in a great increase in man-hour productivity in these and other counties. Only in the middle fifties did most of the new methods spread outside the eastern Pennsylvania, Delaware, and New Jersey farm areas. Even in these advanced counties many farmers resisted change, investing their surplus earnings in land or buildings rather than in improved machinery.

From the long-run economic standpoint, therefore, industrialization in Pennsylvania both in the east and around Pittsburgh was aided in the critical period from 1820 to 1900 by abundant and ever cheaper local food, supplied with greatly increasing efficiency in the use of labor. The gain in productivity per man hour in this period has been estimated at over eighteenfold.

But by the 1870s these increases in efficiency were also taking place on western farms with bigger level acreages, virgin soil, and cheap railroad transportation to eastern markets. On the whole, the mechanization of agriculture and transportation that produced a national market benefited the east-central and west-central states at the expense of farming in the northeast. Consequently, for the Pennsylvania farmer of 1880, profit from grains sold outside his local area were declining or had disappeared. Acreage under cultivation in the commonwealth, which had reached 13.4 million acres on 214,000 farms in 1880, started to contract. Wheat was hardest hit by western competition. In livestock, poultry, truck gardening, and most of all in dairying, Pennsylvania farmers increased production, but these required more capital, labor, and access to nearby markets than had grains.

Between 1860 and 1900 the state shared in the steady increase of government services to agriculture, sometimes in spite of farmer opposition. In 1862 the Morrill Act granted federal land for agricultural education at the rate of 30,000 acres for each congressional representative or senator. While Pennsylvania's share was quickly sold at bargain rates through state politicians, $400,000 was acquired to endow a state agricultural college (now part of Pennsylvania State University). The same session of Congress authorized a federal department of agriculture, which twenty-five years later under the Hatch Act set up state experiment stations. But it was hard to get a semiliterate farmer to experiment systematically, and the state neglected general education. Not until 1874 did the legislature do away with local option and force schools on all the rural townships, while it was 1893 before schooling was made compulsory for children eight to thirteen years old.

Consequently, Pennsylvania farming continued to exemplify almost all stages of agriculture, from advanced dairy, cattle, or truck farms supplying the cities and using up-to-date equipment, to backcountry farms kept nearly self-sufficient by antique practices and the absence of good markets. Industrialization, that is, brought prosperity to the farms that could benefit from feeding nearby industrial workers, but by improving long-distance transportation for western farm products, technical progress made the price of meat, fruit, and grain too low for Pennsylvania farmers in many areas of the state to compete in the larger commercial markets. Gradually, the most depressed agricultural areas lost population as the young people left to take urban jobs, and the land reverted to forest.

Most migrants from farms were, of course, unskilled at urban jobs. The supply of skilled labor depended on either experienced local or immigrant craftsmen. While the latter often had language problems, their relative scarcity kept their wages perhaps fifty percent higher than they could earn in their home countries. Therefore, the American producer tended to think first of the possibility of using more machinery before he advertised for high-priced skilled workers. Even though buying mechanical equipment involved raising and risking more capital, this tendency, which was also well suited to the large mass market, gave the United States superiority in the business use of machine processes.

In addition, industrialists, particularly, feared the unionization of their labor, and machines did not join unions. To most proprietors every aim of worker organizations seemed contrary to managerial authority. Unions tried to prevent promotion on the basis of a foreman's judgment of ability rather than on seniority, demanded shorter hours that could prevent full utilization of a plant, and maintained a steady pressure for maintenance or increase of wages. As the businessman saw it, no plant hampered by union rules could hope to compete with one where management had freedom of operation, and skilled labor was the main type that was unionized.

Outside the skilled crafts, the organization of workers made slow progress in America. But Pennsylvania, as the largest mining and heavy-industry state, was the scene of a number of important and dramatic labor struggles. The chief areas of trouble were not in the old and organized handicraft types of operation where skill was definitely required and apprenticeship enforced, as in leather goods, woodworking, or construction; nor in the textile factories where for all but a few jobs no special skill was needed and organization of the workers had proved impossible; but rather in the rapidly expanding and mechanizing industries such as railroads and metal products where the lines between skill, semiskill, and no skill were hard to draw and continually changing. As an example of this last class of industry, between 1850 and 1875 the four railroad brotherhoods covering the workers who manned the trains were organized, and even without formal employer recognition won concessions, while the railroad shop and yard employees, some of them considerably more skilled than a train brakeman, were not organized, nor, of course, were the white-collar workers who operated the telegraph, sold tickets in stations, or collected freight charges.

The "great railroad strikes" of 1877 may have been lost because of these discrepancies in organization, but they were not a major cause of the initial trouble. Rather the work stoppages were a leaderless, spontaneous resistance by the nonunionized rank and file of railroad workers against continued reductions in pay and increases in work during the long depression. The strikes, occurring on most of the major railroads, reached a maximum of violence in Pittsburgh. The city was by then the largest manufacturing center in the United States that had to rely for its main outflow of traffic on only one railroad—in this case the Pennsylvania. Every local problem in price and wage adjustments came to be blamed by Pittsburgh businessmen on the rates charged by the railroad. Hence when a strike started in the Pittsburgh yards over both pay and reduction of jobs, it received strong support from the other workers in the community. The railroad management, hard-pressed to maintain dividends during the depression, was adamant against any bargaining with the workers. The local militia, called out to guard the yards, was friendly to the men who refused to allow certain trains to be operated. When the governor resorted to elite Philadelphia military units, they were dispersed with bloodshed, and general looting by angry Pittsburgh mobs ensued. Eventually federal troops brought order, and the strikers, lacking experienced local leadership or national organization, gained nothing.

The depression also caused labor trouble in the Pennsylvania hard coal industry. In the mines a degree of experience was needed, but not enough to keep out newcomers. Efforts at unionization, started in 1849, culminated, in 1868, in a Workers Benevolent Association in the anthracite mines, composed of the predominantly Irish workers. The union had to support too many losing strikes, however, particularly in the depression, and in 1875 it disappeared. The activities of the union had also been seriously damaged in the eyes of the nondiscriminating public by an entirely separate secret terrorist organization, the Molly Maguires, which killed a number of mine foremen or supervisors, and was ultimately ended by the arrest and conviction of its leaders.

Before the next period of important union activity, two national organizations had their start chiefly in Pennsylvania. In 1869 a Philadelphia garment-workers' union converted itself into Local Assembly One of the Noble Order of the Knights of Labor. The order organized new chapters on the basis of locality not type of employment, opened membership to self-employed operators and small businessmen, and bound all members to secrecy. The secrecy was valuable during the depression when known union members were likely to be laid off. By the end of 1873 all thirty-one locals of the order were still in the Philadelphia area, where there were separate district assemblies for the two sides of the Delaware. In the ensuing years of depression the organization spread first to Pittsburgh and then to other industrial centers, although the total membership remained small. In 1878 a meeting at Reading set up a national organization of representatives from both district assemblies and individual local chapters. The next year the initial organizer, Uriah Stephens of Philadelphia, resigned, and Terence V. Powderly, third-party mayor of Scranton from 1878 to 1886, became Grand Master Workman for the remaining effective years of the Knights.

Because of strike victories over Western Union and some railroads, the Knights rose briefly to a membership of 600,000 in 1886, but they were never a steadily effective labor organization. "Mixed" locals made up of men from many activities quarreled with trade locals that were basically single-craft unions. Powderly was more interested in political reform, prohibition, and co-operative production than in strikes for better pay or shorter hours. Eventually his group dissipated the funds of the order in unprofitable attempts at production, and during the severe depression of the 1890s the organization ceased to be a force in the labor field.

The other important and more permanent organization of this period grew from a national cigar makers' union engineered by Samuel Gompers and Adolph Strasser in New York City in 1879. After seven years of only moderately successful efforts at broader organization, a Philadelphia conference called for a national organizing meeting at Columbus, Ohio, in December of 1886. At this assembly the American Federation of Labor, composed strictly of craft unions, was organized.

Samuel Gompers became the president, and, except for one two-year term, held the office until his death in 1926. The first important test of the new federation in Pennsylvania was the strike of the Amalgamated Iron, Steel, and Tin Workers at the Carnegie works at Homestead in 1892. In general, even the skilled craftsmen, such as puddlers or molders, were not organized in the newer steel mills, but at Homestead, in a work force of some 4,000, there were nearly 350 members of the Amalgamated. When the Carnegie Company bought the plant in 1889, Henry C. Frick agreed to continue a series of three-year contracts covering the skilled workers, but in the prosperous year of 1892 he refused to agree to a wage increase in a new contract, and the union struck the plant. Carnegie backed Frick, taking the high moral ground that the skilled should not receive treatment that could not be given to the vast majority of their fellow workers. The strike produced a dramatic battle with Pinkerton detectives, an attack on Frick's life by an anarchist not connected with the union, and the exhaustion of the union's resources. This was the first of a series of defeats for unionism in the iron and steel industry prior to 1937.

In the Pennsylvania coal industry organized labor, at the turn of the century, had better success. In 1890 the United Mine Workers were organized from two existing unions, and the new body retained affiliation with both the AFL and the Knights until the latter expelled it in 1894. With the return to prosperity in 1897, the UMW was able to call out 100,000 miners for a strike to restore wages in the central bituminous coalfields of western Pennsylvania and the nearby areas of Ohio, West Virginia, Kentucky, and Tennessee. Wanting to get the benefit of large new orders, the operators gave way, and joined an "Interstate Agreement" establishing the eight-hour day and wages that would equalize production costs throughout an area as far west as Illinois.

The following year a new labor leader, young John Mitchell,

decided that the anthracite fields should also be unionized. Organizing was difficult, as the Irish of the 1870s had been replaced by Italians, Poles, Ruthenians, and other new immigrants, many of whom understood English poorly or not at all. Yet so energetic was the UMW's young Irish president, that by 1900 the unionists felt able to demand a twenty percent wage increase from the operators, who were largely in companies controlled by the railroads. When the union demands were refused, the miners went on strike. Republican political pressure was brought to bear to prevent a prolonged and well-advertised strike of impoverished workingmen in a presidential election year, and a ten percent increase was agreed to.

Neither side was satisfied with the wage compromise, and the operators had not recognized the UMW as a bargaining agent. In May of 1902, when union demands for recognition, higher pay, and the eight-hour day were refused, a new strike was called in the anthracite mines. The strike was well sustained, and by late summer the nation faced an acute winter shortage of coal for heating. At this juncture President Theodore Roosevelt stepped in and demanded arbitration. Pressured by the House of Morgan and other financiers interested in the mine-owning railroads, the operators agreed to arbitration. The award granted a ten-percent wage increase, supervised checking of the weight of coal mined, and security against arbitrary dismissal for union members. Aside from some success in the building trades, these modest victories in the coalfields were the most important achieved before 1910 by the AFL.

The wage increases in mining, exceeding the gradual upswing in the cost of living after 1897, are symbolic of the great underlying change that was occurring in Pennsylvanian and American industrialization. The railroad net had been virtually completed, the chief mining areas had been opened up, the need for new farm housing and equipment was diminishing in relation to the size of the economy while new urban population was tending to use existing buildings more intensively. In a word, capital formation as a percentage of either national or Pennsylvania income was diminishing. If the economy was to function with reasonably full employment, this situation required increasing consumer demand. Thus the mild rise of successful unionism at the turn of the century can be seen as an element in forcing businessmen, whose ideas of efficiency ran contrary to voluntary increases in wages to give workmen a bigger share in growing consumption.

In the large readjustments of population, agriculture, and working conditions in the late nineteenth century, the commonwealth government played a relatively minor role. Perhaps it is more realistic to say that the new industrialists found little need to change the practices of government. While there was never any real doubt that the state government was controlled by politicians supported financially by many businessmen, entrepreneurs as a group were not united on positive governmental policies or willing to take an active part in politics. What battles there were in state politics went on over issues that businessmen regarded as either relatively unimportant or somebody else's concern. "Reform" meant appointing honest men to jobs, making "bad" corporations obey the law, and curtailing the increase in state offices or the size of the debt. In other words, making the existing government perform with reasonable efficiency. In this the views of Pennsylvanians prior to 1900 were not different from those of the people of other eastern states. During the nationwide movement for progressive reforms, from about 1900 to 1915, however, Pennsylvanians remained reasonably content with the status quo and responded slowly to the pressures for more government regulation.

In the immediate post-Civil War period the state was run by United States Senator Simon Cameron, who in 1872 and 1873 sponsored a very conservative convention, which drew up a new constitution. Some of the members of the convention, such as Franklin B. Gowen of the Reading Railroad and Philadelphia sugar refiner E. C. Knight, were important businessmen; many others were lawyers; only one was a farmer; and nobody represented labor. The Pittsburgh Gazette reported: "In respect of wealth it is the heaviest deliberative body that ever met in Pennsylvania. . . . No trifling with the conservative principles of society here." [2]

2. Quoted from Philip S. Klein and Ari Hoogenboom, *A History of Pennsylvania* (New York: McGraw Hill, 1973), p. 319.

Reactionary or not, the constitution ratified in 1874 lasted unchanged for ninety-five years. In fact, it included many provisions designed to lessen bad practices. Legislative procedures, for example, were altered to prevent the flood of private acts that had recently outnumbered general bills by nearly twenty to one. In the future, special charters could not be enacted for nonexistent corporations, as with the Tom Scott companies. To make corruption more costly, the house and senate were greatly increased in size, and representation was made more uniform. Elaborate stipulations sought to secure fiscal honesty and prevent reckless accumulation of debt. It was on the surface a good, businesslike document, designed to check malpractices in a conservative government. Since in the long run no change in the general political attitudes of the controlling middle class of the state followed the enactment of the new constitution, the document made little difference in political practices. Business leaders, having exerted themselves to reform the government, now returned to commercial affairs and left politics to politicians.

For the next twenty years although the successive Republican machines run by Cameron and then by Mathew Quay were generally dominant, there was some effective Democratic opposition. Robert E. Pattison, a Democrat, was elected governor in 1882 and again in 1890, and Democrat William A. Wallace was United States senator from 1875 to 1881. But the Democrats lacked strong support from industrial labor because of their weakness on the tariff issue, antiunionism, and general conservatism. From 1894 on to 1936, no Democrat was elected governor or United States senator.

The Republican machine was built on control of the local townships, cities, and counties. The bosses at these levels were rewarded by receiving state or federal offices that were sinecures, and they in turn got out the vote, using as many repeaters as necessary. The whole structure was so complex—including complicated city machines in Pittsburgh and Philadelphia and often containing conflicting interests—that the state boss was as much run by the needs of the machine as was the machine run by him. As Boies Penrose, the dominant state boss from 1904 on, told a group of businessmen, he would do the best he could for them, but he, not they, knew what was possible and what was not. Leadership in Pennsylvania meant keeping the party organization functioning reasonably smoothly in all of its diverse parts.

Utility companies and those involved in public construction had, of course, to keep particularly close to the dominant state and local machines. For example, starting with horsecar lines in 1881, Mathew Quay, William H. Kemble, and Peter A. B. Widener, all connected with the state Republican machine, strove for a monopoly of Philadelphia traction. The legislature, of course, passed all necessary laws, but the politicians quarreled among themselves. The result was more companies, new insiders, William L. Elkins and Peter Dolan in place of Kemble and Quay, and ultimately a compromise in 1902 in the form of a greatly overcapitalized monopoly: the Philadelphia Rapid Transit Company.

Such politically facilitated deals at the expense of taxpayers and consumers had become familiar to Philadelphians. By the late 1860s the gas company, taken over by the city in 1841, was run as a patronage and money base by corrupt Republican city bosses. The hold of the machine was, no doubt, facilitated by the relative decline in the proportion of Quakers in the population and a large increase in the foreign-born. In addition both Hicksite and Orthodox Quakers (they had split in 1827) were generally Republicans and subscribed to the Books of Discipline that admonished "all in profession with us to decline any office or station in civil government, the duties of which are inconsistent with our religious principles." [3] Since practically all offices involved sanctioning military or violent action, most Quakers avoided participation in politics. At a peak of corruption in the late 1870s, described by James Bryce in the *American Commonwealth*, some important Quakers such as T. Wistar Brown did join with a reform committee of one hundred to elect Democrat S. G. King mayor in 1881, but reformist zeal seems never to have lasted long in Philadelphia or most other large American cities.

3. Ralph S. Benjamin, *The Philadelphia Quakers in the Industrial Age* (Philadelphia: Temple University Press, 1976), p. 74.

Whether corrupt or honest, government in Pennsylvania was probably less affected by industrialization than governments in Britain or western Europe, though the lives of the people may have undergone more change. Except for New York, no state of similar size in America or abroad was so deluged with immigrants from 1845 to 1910. Consequently, Pennsylvania not only underwent the upheavals in life-styles everywhere attendant on the sudden growth of railroads, factories, and big cities, but also those associated with the acculturation of large numbers of people speaking foreign languages. As a result, Pennsylvania of 1910 was a state of extreme contrasts between old, rather unchanged German or Scotch-Irish farming areas, much wilderness of second growth timber, and heavily foreign, unplanned, and unregulated industrial centers. From a province with no city of 20,000 people in 1760, in a hundred and fifty years the state had come to have a metropolitan area at Philadelphia of over two million and one at Pittsburgh half that large. From the standpoint of making the United States a world leader through the production of iron and steel, the development of Pennsylvania before World War I had been an outstanding national success. From the standpoint of good living for the majority of its own citizens, the results were more mixed.

10

Pennsylvania in the Twentieth Century

IN the last half of the twentieth century, Pennsylvania may again be one of the foremost states leading in a direction that western Europe has already taken and that the United States, it appears, will have to follow. The industrialized state or nation of the next century may have slowly growing or stationary population, highly capitalized agriculture conducted by relatively few farmers, medium-sized manufacturing plants located in rural or urban fringe areas with a declining number of workers, many more non-farm families living in the country, and much employment in recreation, serving travelers, maintaining transportation, or repairing increasingly complex consumer goods. In most of these respects change was well advanced in Pennsylvania by 1976.

The state also shared largely in the changes in movements of population brought about by federal policies. During the period of relatively unrestricted immigration before World War I, people from Europe continued to flow into the state and seek jobs in mining or industry. War stopped the flow, and federal laws from 1921 on prevented its resumption on the old levels. Meanwhile, booming industry had found a partial substitute for immigrant labor in the thousands of blacks migrating from the rural south. But the latter movement was on a smaller scale than

178

the great flow from eastern Europe before the war. Up to 1910 the total population of the state had grown 20 percent or more each decade. From 1920 to 1930 it grew only 10½ percent, well below the national average, and from 1960 to 1970, only 4 percent in a decade when the nation grew by over 13 percent.

In remaining a state manufacturing an unusual amount of durable goods or heavy industrial products, Pennsylvania was linked to its past. Like Britain in the history of the industrialization of the western world, Pennsylvania gradually came to have equals among the other states in coal and steel; unlike Britain, this was not because Pennsylvania's mining or manufacturing started to lag, but because, from 1915 on, production in California, Illinois, Michigan, and Ohio grew with great rapidity. The remarkable thing is that this oldest center of heavy industry was, in 1970, still among the first half-dozen states in mineral production, value added by manufacture and value of goods shipped. In coal production Pennsylvania was exceeded only by West Virginia and Kentucky, and there were still great deposits of anthracite and bituminous in its historic mining areas. In cement making the state was surpassed only by California. In 1971 only Texas, a latecomer, exceeded Pennsylvania in capital expenditures for manufacturing.

In spite of preserving its older patterns of mining and industry, Pennsylvania was also caught up in the sweeping technological changes of the twentieth century that led to social changes on a par with those wrought by factories and railroads a hundred years earlier. Electricity, automotive transportation by land and air, scientific knowledge and self-powered machinery applied to agriculture, and facilities for long-term financing of the small buyer, all altered ways of living and working.

Steam had been most efficient in large factories where machinery was connected to a big central engine by belts and shafts, but electricity was practically as efficient in operating a single hand tool as in powering a big plant. This meant that in the matter of fabrication itself, the small shop could compete with the large one, and that new products might be launched on a small scale. The fact that in 1974 there were 16,749 manufacturing establishments in Pennsylvania illustrates this diffusion of production. Since electric power lines and highways criss-crossed the state and trucks distributed products, factories no longer had to be near coal, oil, or railroads.

The great rise of the automotive industry from 1920 on produced a situation that contrasted with that of the earlier railroads. While the railroads had been assisted by public loans, they planned and owned their tracks. In contrast, the automobile and truck were only usable when the government supplied roads. In other words, the automotive industry was what economists would call a "mixed" one, in which private enterprise made the equipment and government supplied the larger share of "overhead capital." Therefore the twentieth-century revolution in transportation involved large sums, federal, state, and local, for highway construction, part of which were recovered in gasoline and license taxes. Inevitably there were legislative contests over where the money would be spent.

The freeing of industry from railroad transportation and pools of big city labor occurred rapidly after World War II. While the new society of dispersed small plants drawing workers by private automobile from the surrounding countryside was widely predicted in 1920, poor highways, and then a decade of depression slowed the change, while World War II further delayed normal patterns of redistribution. Consequently, the new world of the small rural factory came suddenly in the years after 1945, checking the growth of cities and transforming the nearby countryside. The small operator or worker was also aided in buying automobiles, business equipment, and housing by veterans' benefits and long-term financing through both banks and commercial credit companies. Federally guaranteed mortgages, available for nearly all of the cost of inexpensive houses, made Pennsylvania a state of home owners.

The same lag followed by an explosive outburst occurred in the application of scientific knowledge and light machinery to agriculture. From the twenties on, agro-biologists had developed hybrid seeds for grain, better feeding and selection systems for poultry and cattle, and new possibilities in fertilization and pest control. In the 1930s the big, heavy tractors of the previous decade were replaced by small, relatively inexpensive gasoline-powered machines that could be used efficiently on moderate acreages. By 1940 the array of new machines was bewildering even to specialists in the Department of Agriculture. But farmers were not inclined to experiment or invest money during the depression, particularly since they were being paid to limit production of staple crops. It took the excessive demands of World War II to end the period of stagnation and suddenly put all the new ideas, practices, and machines into use. The result over the next twenty-five years was the most rapid change in methods in the history of world agriculture, the so-called "green revolution." From 1950 to 1966, for example, productivity per worker in manufacturing increased 50 percent; in farming the figure was 150 percent, and if only large-scale commercial farming—equivalent to factory industry—had been measured, the increase would have been much greater.

The new highly productive agriculture required capital, knowledge, and a sizable agreage. Consequently, while total Pennsylvania farm income rose to new heights, partly from inflation, the number of farms leveled off at about 70,000 in 1965 and remained nearly stationary for the next decade, even though total state population rose slightly. Put as a percentage of population, the long-run change is even more striking. In 1880, at the peak of independent farming in Pennsylvania, operating farmers were 5 percent of the population; in 1975 they were a little over half of one percent. Each individual farm, however, averaging 145 acres, was larger than ever before.

Since western pressures on eastern farming were already present in 1880, the shift in types of product was small. At the earlier date farmers had still marketed some grains, beside dairy products and animals. In recent years dairying has been the largest source of income with eggs and beef running neck and neck for second and third places. Fertile fields still yielded large grain crops, but they were were used for feeding local farm animals. Reflecting a swing toward truck farming, fruits, and specialties (such as cut flowers), the state led the nation in the production of mushrooms.

Yet, even though commercial farmers were two-thirds fewer than in the late nineteenth century, the countryside was far from deserted. In 1970, omitting the two completely urban counties of Allegheny (Pittsburgh) and Philadelphia, the remaining 65 counties averaged 125,000 people. Of these 25 counties had less than 50,000 people, but all except seven of the small counties were more populous than they had been in 1890, just after the peak of farm development. And among the seven small counties there were four that had always been mainly mountains and forest. Thus, in spite of the growth of some major cities, rural Pennsylvania had not become depopulated, but the occupations of people in the country had changed greatly.

The process of change can be illustrated from historian John Shover's analysis of Bedford County.[1] Situated midway along the southern border, the town of Bedford, the county seat, was on the old southern highway from Lancaster, York, and Chambersburg to Pittsburgh, often called Forbes Road in honor of that general's triumphant march to Fort Duquesne in 1758. In 1890 the population of Bedford County was 39,000 and in 1970, 44,000; in other words, it remained practically stationary. At both periods the people were predominantly white and native-born. While some coal and iron mining went on until 1930, the county had never had a mining boom to draw in immigrants, or cities to provide work for blacks from the south. At both periods dairy farming was important, but the 3,500 farms of 1890 had diminished to under 1,300 by 1970, and only 786 workers claimed agriculture as their principal activity.

Turnpike service and rural manufacturing had provided jobs for the men and women displaced by the revolution in agricultural technology. From 1940 to 1965, Breezewood, just north of the county seat, benefited increasingly from being a repair and rest stop on the Pennsylvania Turnpike. Just as the railroads had earlier built Altoona and Johnstown, the turnpike brought light industry and service to Bedford. Like most of the rural counties, Bedford offered industry nonunion labor supplied largely from local people no longer needed on farms. In the late 1960s, new Interstate 80 drew away some of the turnpike traffic, but

1. John Shover, *First Majority Last Minority: The Transformation of Rural Life in America* (De Kalb: Northern Illinois University Press, 1976), pp. 81–107.

Breezewood remained a collection of motels and service stations. Meanwhile employment in recreation services had developed from the nineteenth century on. South of Bedford town there were mineral springs and hotels that continued to attract conventions and upper-income visitors in the summer, while a nearby ski resort, Blue Knob, attracted vacationers in the winter.

None of the new activities built up cities. In 1970 the county was classed by the federal census as 92 percent rural. But only a little over 10 percent of the rural people were on operating farms. The others lived in new rural developments, scattered new country homes, or previously abandoned farmhouses. Some of the new manufacturing establishments drew two hundred or more workers from the surrounding countryside. Yet, as in many of the other rural counties of both Pennsylvania and the northeastern states in general, the situation in the 1970s was not one of satisfactory adjustment to the forces of change. In the depression year of 1975 unemployment in Bedford County ran over 12 percent as against 9.6 percent for the state as a whole, and the Penn Central Railroad had asked to discontinue the branch line to Altoona.

This one rather poorly located rural county, however, gives a false impression of employment in the state as a whole. The labor force all over the nation was growing more rapidly than the population. Between 1960 and 1970 Pennsylvania's population rose only 4 percent, while nonagricultural employment increased by 17 percent. Employment in agriculture was already so low that its small drop during the period scarcely registered in the overall statistics. In addition to jobs being more plentiful in relation to the total population, most work was physically easier and the hours much shorter than at the start of the century. Then a 60-hour week was the rule, instead of the 40 hours or less of the 1970s. Small manufacturing plants with good lighting, adequate sanitary facilities, and a country setting compared favorably with the big, dirty factory operations in the rundown urban areas of the earlier years of the century. The world wars, the spread of white-collar jobs, the labor shortages from 1945 to 1957, and fair-employment laws had brought an increasingly large percentage of women into the labor force. In some families men were unemployed but women worked; and while in the nineteenth century two workers per household may have been necessary for a decent living, in the relative affluence of the late twentieth century one worker might provide what an earlier age would have regarded as luxury. This level of living included not only the essential automobile, which gave a freedom of movement unthought of earlier, but also, to people in Bedford County, home entertainment by cable television from Washington, Baltimore, Philadelphia, and Pittsburgh. The latter facility depended on the electrification of country homes, which had been started during the New Deal, and was virtually accomplished in the state by 1975.

Although the general shift of American population southward was having a depressing long-run effect on all northern areas, the problems of the state's two big cities were more severe than those in the country. Up to 1920 both Pittsburgh and Philadelphia had continued to grow rapidly, in part from European immigration up to 1914, and after that from black workers and families drawn from the rural south. Even though total in-city population leveled off after 1930, the two centers, particularly Philadelphia, continued to attract blacks. Meanwhile native white residents were moving to the suburbs. As a result Philadelphia, which had a black population of only 4.8 percent in 1900 was 33.6 percent black in 1970. The large northeastern area of the city, with well over a quarter of the population and much of the manufacturing, was almost completely white, which meant that in some other sections non-whites ran over 70 percent. Since unemployment was substantially higher among blacks than whites, housing in the heavily black areas tended to deteriorate, and the homes of people who had gone elsewhere remained empty.

Although population growth slowed down in the twentieth century, the state remained in 1970 the third largest in the Union, but with Texas and Illinois close behind and growing faster. Only California's two metropolitan areas, Los Angeles (number two) and San Francisco-Oakland (number six) combined, ranked further up the national list than Philadelphia and

Pittsburgh, at number four and number eleven respectively. Almost ninety percent of the people of the state lived in "standard metropolitan areas," although the title is somewhat misleading as an "area" may include much open country. One of the oddest "standard areas" in the nation was "Northeast Pennsylvania" with a 1970 population of 632,000 and a national rank of 56. It is actually comprised of three counties—Monroe, Lackawanna, and Luzerne—that include many square miles of state parks and the Pocono Mountains in addition to the cities of Hazleton, Scranton, and Wilkes-Barre, with Hazleton at the southern end, twenty country miles from its nearest central city neighbor.

The flight of manufacturing to the country, as seen in Bedford, tended to undermine the old big cities closely built around factories. Furthermore, total employment in manufacturing has been declining, while the most rapid increases have been in specialized services. Since Pittsburgh as an industrial center was built up by the exploitation of now diminishing local resources, the decline has been more dramatic there than in Philadelphia, which depended on a mixture of light industry, trade, and service. Big companies based in Pittsburgh continued to grow through expansion to nearby rural areas and diversification of products, but their work force in the city decreased. This has had the effect of maintaining the Golden Triangle as a major financial center, behind only New York, Chicago, and San Francisco in nonlocal loans, while between 1960 and 1970 Pittsburgh was losing over 10 percent of its population. In the 1970s the metropolitan area was also declining, but at a very moderate rate. In contrast, while Philadelphia as a city lost 2.5 percent in population during the sixties, the metropolitan area continued slowly to grow until the mid-seventies. Of the nation's twenty largest cities, all the older ones, except New York and Memphis, lost population in the 1960s.

In spite of having fewer employed workers, the cities have not lost importance as business centers, and in Pennsylvania the larger ones have made some striking downtown improvements. Allentown, for example, Pennsylvania's fourth largest city, has glass-covered shopping malls running for several blocks on both sides of its main street. Philadelphia and the Pennsylvania Railroad co-operated in the 1950s to put the entire midcity passenger operation underground, making way for a new two-block-wide and seven-block-long area of glass and steel skyscrapers, as well as a more impressive city hall plaza. Up to 1973, at least, construction of new central city office buildings went on rapidly in all of the nation's largest centers.

Perhaps nowhere have the results of planned improvement been more dramatic than in Pittsburgh. The so-called renaissance of the downtown area has a long background. A severe flood in 1936 damaged much of the triangular business district between the rivers. To induce new business and rebuilding, the president of the Mellon National Bank, Richard K. Mellon, joined with Mayor David L. Lawrence in a campaign to create conditions attractive to investors in business construction. The first step, initiated in the late thirties, was to get the state, with federal assistance, to build dams that would end the periodic flooding of the lower Allegheny and Monongahela. The next step was an ordinance forbidding the burning of soft coal within the city. Not enforced until the end of the wartime shortage of fuel, this was a very important factor in making the downtown area attractive for business purposes. Finally, after World War II, state laws gave the city the right of eminent domain for condemnation and rebuilding and, in 1956, set up a Pennsylvania Industrial Development Authority to make loans for expanding or establishing new businesses in areas of high unemployment.

The factual details fail to do justice to the enthusiasm for rebuilding generated by Mellon and Lawrence in the postwar years. Within about a decade a business district of discolored old buildings was transformed into one of glass and steel. Old bridges were replaced with attractive new ones, and an extremely complex system of limited-access highways kept much of the traffic off the streets. Few cities in the United States, or the world for that matter, present more pleasing and exciting views than those of the Golden Triangle, with the wide rivers and steep hills framing green parks and modern skyscrapers.

Improvements in the outward aspects of industrial centers was matched by better conditions of work and ultimately by more harmonious and orderly labor relations. Until after World War I the great majority of steelworkers put in a twelve-hour day and were not represented by any union. The old Amalgamated Iron, Steel, and Tin Workers, after losing a badly run strike in 1901, had declined to a membership of only a few thousand. An effort at organization on an industrial, noncraft basis in 1919 and 1920 failed after a prolonged strike. In 1923 the steel companies, partly in response to adverse public opinion and political pressure, voluntarily granted the eight-hour day with a 25 percent hourly-wage increase.

In spite of an industrial type of organization from its beginning in the nineteenth century, the United Mine Workers were unsuccessful in unionizing the coal companies. Unlike the steel industry, where domestic prices were controlled by tacit agreements among a handful of big companies, after World War I bituminous coal operators were numerous, and prices were declining. The result was wage cutting and desperate, generally futile strikes in protest. Although John L. Lewis and his UMW had the sympathy of Gifford Pinchot, governor from 1923 to 1927, the union ended the decade with an exhausted treasury and a long record of failure.

The period of the New Deal, starting in 1933, brought a revolutionary and lasting change in American labor relations. By the National Labor Relations Act of 1935, generally called the Wagner Act, union organizers were not only granted protection to enter plants and talk to the workers, but the employers were forbidden to discourage this activity in any way. When the union thought that it had the support of a majority of the workers, it could call for an election, supervised by the National Labor Relations Board. If it won a majority of the votes in the election, all employees had to join the union, and the company had to deduct dues from paychecks. To the consternation of businessmen and most politicians, the United States Supreme Court in April of 1937 held the law to be a constitutional exercise of the federal power over interstate commerce.

Meanwhile, John L. Lewis had seized the opportunity to lead a Congress for Industrial Organizations that had set up noncraft unions in eight industries by 1936, when the group was expelled from the AFL. The re-election of Franklin D. Roosevelt by a landslide in 1936 encouraged the new industrial unions to swing into action. The most spectacular strikes were in the rubber and automobile industries in Michigan and Ohio, where the French device of the sit-down strike (the workers staying in the plant) was effectively used. In the General Motors strikes President Roosevelt gave strong support to Lewis, as head of the CIO; this, together with the control of local affairs by a prolabor governor of Michigan, forced the company to give in to the demands of the union.

A strong demand for steel in the spring of 1937 and the example of General Motors' defeat, led Myron C. Taylor, president of United States Steel to voluntarily enter into a contract with the Steel Workers Organizing Committee of the CIO. The other steel companies, however, refused to follow his lead, and violent labor troubles continued in Pennsylvania until the early 1940s, when the National Labor Relations Board backed by the Supreme Court forced recognition of the union.

From World War II on, American labor has been about 25 percent unionized, but most of the organized workers have been in industry, where, after 1953, total employment was declining. By spreading into trade and service, particularly in transportation and government, unions have been able to maintain a fairly uniform degree of organization among the growing numbers of employed workers. For example, Governor Shapp, acting under the Pennsylvania Public Employees Relations Act of 1970, entered into a contract with 17,500 highway workers who were members of the American Federation of State, County and Municipal Employees.

Pennsylvania, one of the major producers of fuel and heavy durable goods, has been more seriously affected by wars and depressions than have the states involved to a greater extent in trade and light industry. In World War I, the Pittsburgh area, supplying 80 percent of the steel for munitions, was called the "arsenal of the world." Charles M. Schwab as chairman of the Emergency Fleet Corporation built the Hog Island Shipyard south of Philadelphia that started construction on hundreds of freighters. In all, special war plants in the state employed half a million additional workers.

The Great Depression of the 1930s had, of course, a severe opposite effect. Few firms or governments needed the products of heavy industry. The great Baldwin Locomotive Works at Philadelphia made just four engines in 1932. Unemployment in some mining or steel towns ran about 80 percent, and before the institution of federal relief in 1933 there were deaths from starvation. While New Deal agencies such as Emergency Relief and the Works Progress Administration helped to alleviate the most severe suffering, only preparation for World War II ended the depression.

As in World War I, the second global conflict greatly stimulated Pennsylvanian mining and industry, but the boom was shared with other states. Although Pennsylvania remained second in total manufacturing, it ranked seventh in war contracts. The Korean and Vietnamese wars also aided heavy industry and brought prosperity. With periods of war and peace of roughly equal duration from 1941 to 1972, Pennsylvania's traditional manufacturing did well, and this also helped to stimulate much new light industry, trade, and service. In the prosperity of the middle 1960s, aided by the state development authority, which helped new firms, the rate of unemployment fell to under 3 percent, one percentage point below that of the nation as a whole.

But with the spread of people and transportation across the continent Pennsylvania could never expect to regain its old dominance. Companies—many of which had originated in the state—became so large that they began producing and selling from plants and branches located all over the nation. They tended to shift head offices to the three major regional centers, New York, Chicago, and Los Angeles. A goodly number of such giants in manufacturing, trade, and service, however, still have their home offices in Philadelphia or Pittsburgh. Of the fifty largest manufacturing corporations rated by sales in *Fortune* Pittsburgh is the home of four: Gulf Oil, United States Steel, Westinghouse, and Rockwell International; while Du Pont, Sun Oil, and Bethlehem Steel are headquartered near Philadelphia. Aside from Los Angeles, also with four companies, no city other than Chicago or New York equaled Pittsburgh's concentration of the biggest companies, and only New York State exceeded the two Pennsylvania metropolitan areas in the concentration of head offices of the fifty biggest manufacturing firms. In the field of finance the Mellon National Corporation in Pittsburgh is the nation's fifteenth largest banker, and four of the fifty largest firms have their headquarters in Philadelphia. Among "diversified financial companies" rated by assets, Insurance Company of North America in Philadelphia is twelfth and Equimark of Pittsburgh, nineteenth.

The Philadelphia Stock Exchange, oldest in the nation, expanded greatly in the twentieth century. In 1931 the governing board of this exchange initiated the trading of all stocks listed on the New York Stock Exchange, the Curb (later American) Exchange, and the Boston, Chicago, and Pittsburgh exchanges. It took ten years for the New York Stock Exchange to accept this invasion of its list, but under pressure from the Securities and Exchange Commission, the New Yorkers finally did. Starting in 1949, by a series of mergers and associate membership agreements, the Philadelphia exchange became the leader of the east coast outside of New York. First it merged with the Baltimore exchange and then with the Washington exchange. Merger with Pittsburgh in 1969 started the system of dual trading floors in the two cities. This principle was extended in 1974 in a merger with the Southeastern Stock Exchange in Miami. Meanwhile, in 1972 the affiliates adopted the name PWB Stock Exchange, Inc. This whole movement, which helped to preserve the financial importance of these regional centers, illustrated the possibilities of improved electrical communication for decentralized business.

Three retailing chains each with over a billion dollars in sales are centered in the Philadelphia area, American Stores, Food Fair Stores, and ARA Services, but on the basis of the nineteenth-century history of Pennsylvania, as compared to New York, Illinois, or California, one would not expect a concentration of trade or transportation equal to that of finance and heavy industry. In fact, emphasis on big corporations gives a false impression of the business of any state or nation. The two or three thousand really large companies of the United States employ only about a quarter of all workers, and occupy the time of a much smaller percentage of all businessmen. Pennsylvania's proprietorships and partnerships, 450,000 in 1970, have always carried on most of the business of the state. And in the numbers and income of such small to medium-sized factories, shops, banks, and other services, Pennsylvania has maintained a place within the top half-dozen states.

The Pennsylvania Railroad, with its headquarters in Philadelphia, had been the nation's largest for over a century, and it was still larger by merger with the New York Central in 1968. The resulting Penn Central with a management divided between New York and Philadelphia, poorly co-ordinated operations, overly generous treatment of excess labor, and weak executives at the top, quickly accumulated large debts. A severe winter and a downturn in the business cycle put the company into bankruptcy in the spring of 1970. It now forms a part of CONRAIL, the federally funded corporation responsible for the operation of a number of financially troubled eastern railroads.

There was no great change in the basic relations of business with politics in the commonwealth during the first third of the twentieth century. Although Pennsylvania adopted a child-labor law in 1905, restricted working hours for women in 1913, and made workmen's compensation compulsory in 1915, all over persistent business opposition, there was no strong progressive movement in state politics. It seems rather that legal action came because working conditions were becoming too bad, particularly in the mines, to be tolerated by American democratic society.

The reforms were enacted while Boies Penrose, a highly cultivated gentleman, was running the state from his seat in the United States Senate. When Penrose died unexpectedly in 1921, his power was divided between the Mellon interests in Pittsburgh, William S. Vare's machine in Philadelphia, and Joseph R. Grundy, whose strength rested upon the influence of the Pennsylvania Association of Manufacturers. Since there had never been a Republican policy as such, other than a general reluctance to go contrary to the wishes of business, division of authority in the state apparently made little difference in practice, but division within the party did permit the election in 1922 of Gifford Pinchot, a reformer, as governor.

Pinchot, a member of a wealthy family from Milford on the upper Delaware River, served as Director of Forestry in the Theodore Roosevelt and Taft administrations and became a nationally famous conservationist. While he ran for governor on a conservative platform and appeared to have had no advanced ideas regarding reform in general, he was an honest, self-assured autocrat who worried machine politicians. Had not the constitution of 1873 prohibited the governor from succeeding himself, Pinchot with popular support might have built a strong liberal Republican machine. But because of this provision, no chief executive was able to build control of the state around his office. The best resource, at the end of a term as governor, was to run for the United States Senate. Cameron, Quay, and Penrose had all run the state in this capacity. By 1930, however, the senatorial patronage had been eroded by the spread of classified federal civil service, whereas that of the governor had grown greatly. Consequently, no succeeding state boss has been able to "rule from Washington." Pinchot, however, did not have a chance to try. The divisions within the Republican party now defeated him in his bid for nomination for the Senate race.

The varying balances of power within the party made all nominations uncertain. Continuing friction between the Vare and Grundy forces in 1930 allowed Pinchot to again win the governorship. This administration, even more than his first, demonstrated the difficulty of the governor commanding a majority of the legislature for any liberal program. Except for the State Emergency Relief Board, the Pinchot administration failed to persuade the legislature to pass any New Deal legislation. The first Roosevelt administration had little effect on Pennsylvania.

In the widespread Republican defeat of 1934, the Democrats elected George M. Earl as governor and Joseph F. Guffey as United States senator. But since only half the state senators were up for re-election, the Republicans retained a majority in that house, which blocked most of Earl's proposals until the still more sweeping Democratic victories of 1936. In the final two years of his term Earl implemented within the state the labor and social security programs of the New Deal. Regardless of the party in power, relief or work programs of all types were openly administered for political ends.

In 1938, with Roosevelt's popularity at a low ebb, the Republicans resumed their control of the state. But since both Pittsburgh and Philadelphia were now likely to produce Democratic majorities, the Republicans were never as secure as they had been before 1934. On the whole, Republican and occasional Democratic administrations moved in the directions that have seemed inevitable in the modern industrial state. More state agencies were added, while highway construction and education, particularly, increased the number of employees and the size of the state budget. In 1919 state expenditures were $50 million, and there were 2,710 employees. In 1950 the annual budget had risen to $500 million, in dollars worth a little less than in 1919, and employees numbered 59,000; by 1970 the budget had climbed to $3.3 billion in dollars worth about half as much as in 1919, and state employees had risen to 110,000.

Meanwhile, the strength of the Democratic vote in both Philadelphia and Pittsburgh had made Pennsylvania a fairly evenly balanced two-party state. Both parties lacked powerful state bosses, and men such as Democrat Milton E. Shapp could win the governorship in 1970 in spite of opposition or cool support by the city machines. Shapp's administrations marked a major change in governmental functioning. In 1968, a constitutional convention, the first since 1873, struck out the clause prohibiting the governor from succeeding himself, and Shapp was able to create a continuing political organization based in Harrisburg, which helped re-elect him in 1974. Since Shapp was a former businessman, his administration was not particularly interested in further regulation, but he did find it necessary to push through a 2.3 percent uniform income tax in order to postpone a further increase in sales and property taxes, which could drive away business. One might conclude that the government of Pennsylvania was still strongly pro-business, but was finding it necessary to institute new taxes in order to meet the high costs of welfare and a continually more expensive state bureaucracy. To meet these expenses, which were growing the fastest of any costs of government in all the leading industrial states, the increasing numbers of employed workers at all levels of income were taxed more to carry the burden of expanding public services.

Since employment opportunities were shifting from those in industry, or in jobs needing only unskilled labor toward those in service, requiring some special training, many of the unemployed of 1976 might not be rehired. Increasing automation in manufacturing and use of the computer for office work were bringing about the service society in the western world, including Pennsylvania, and business innovations were needed to create more jobs in fields such as maintenance, travel, and recreation.

The inherited belief that only fabrication was productive made it hard for many people to visualize a society based chiefly on service. Even economists were inclined carelessly to equate manufacturing with production, to see a new automobile, for example, as an addition to national wealth, but not the repair work that might prolong the useful life of the vehicle. Similarly construction workers would be regarded as producers, but not the plumbers or painters that kept the building functioning properly. At all events, Pennsylvania with a disproportionally large number of workers employed in companies carrying on fabrication, would have more difficulty in adjusting to the changing order than would states already having a larger percentage of workers in trade or service. Historically such challenges have been a cause of innovation, and since Pennsylvania was facing the greatest problems, it might become a leader in new solutions.

In spite of serious readjustments in jobs and the gradual movement of all types of work to rural areas, the country of rolling hills, winding river valleys and heavily wooded mountain ranges seen by the early colonists had changed less than in most eastern states. The large total acreage of Pennsylvania and the concentration of 10½ million of its 12 million people in a dozen metropolitan areas has left most of the state looking much as it did in colonial times. State parks insure the permanence of forests and wildlife, but since the end of the initial timber-cutting period, now more than a century ago, much of the northern and western regions has never again been invaded by either intensive agriculture or industry. With manufacturing in the future employing a smaller part of a more stable national population, Penn's "greene" province, if not his "countrie town" on the Delaware, may remain, with pleasing contrasts between the highest levels of industrial enterprise in a few centers and a vast surrounding backcountry that has largely reverted to its seventeenth-century appearance.

Suggestions for Further Reading

Textbooks dealing with the general history of the state do not add much to the descriptions of early industrial development presented here. One of the best and most recent of such volumes is *A History of Pennsylvania* by Philip S. Klein and Ari Hoogenboom (New York: McGraw-Hill, 1973). The colonial cities and their business are covered in four well-written and scholarly volumes by Carl Bridenbaugh, of which *Cities in Revolt: Urban Life in America 1743–1776* (New York: Capricorn, 1964) was the most useful for this book. For the great period of Philadelphia finance, Bray Hammond's *Banks and Politics in America: from the Revolution to the Civil War* (Princeton: Princeton University Press, 1957) is both the pleasantest to read and the most generally informing. Victor S. Clark, *History of Manufactures in the United States*, 3 vols. (New York: McGraw-Hill, 1929) is necessarily much concerned with Pennsylvania. The same may be said of George R. Taylor's scholarly and interesting *The Transportation Revolution 1815–1860* (New York: Holt, Rinehart and Winston, 1962).

An original and discerning view of the conditions of eastern settlement and early development is James T. Lemon's *The Best Poor Man's Country: A Geographical Study of Early Southern Pennsylvania* (Baltimore: Johns Hopkins University Press, 1972). For an interpretation of the physical details of early Philadelphia see Sam B. Warner, *The Private City: Philadelphia in Three Periods of its Growth* (Philadelphia: University of Pennsylvania Press, 1968) and for many excellent essays on buildings Luther P. Eisenhart, editor, *Historic Philadelphia: From the Founding to the Early Nineteenth Century* (Philadelphia: American Philosophical Society, Transactions, no. 43, part I, 1953). Warner's discussion of the early merchants is given greater depth and detail in Clarence Ver Steeg, *Robert Morris: Revolutionary Financier* (Philadelphia: University of Pennsylvania Press, 1954) and Edwin T. Wolf II and Maxwell Whitman, *The History of*

For Further Reading

the Jews of Philadelphia from Colonial Times to the Age of Jackson (Philadelphia: The Jewish Publication Society of America, 1957). A careful and penetrating study by Stephanie Grauman Wolf, *An Urban Village: Population, Community and Family Structure in Germantown, Pennsylvania* (Princeton: Princeton University Press, 1976) suggests much of the social and economic history of the other satellite cities.

General background on the rivalry of Baltimore, New York, and Philadelphia can be acquired from the essays in David T. Gilchrist, ed., *The Growth of the Seaport Cities, 1790–1825* (Charlottesville: University Press of Virginia, for Eleutherian Mills–Hagley Foundation, 1967); from geographer Allan R. Pred, *Urban Growth and the Circulation of Information: The United States System of Cities, 1790–1840* (Cambridge: Harvard University Press, 1973); from Leighton P. Stradley, *Early Financial and Economic History of Pennsylvania* (New York: Commerce Clearing House, 1942); and from James Weston Livingood, *The Philadelphia-Baltimore Trade Rivalry, 1780–1860* (Harrisburg: Pennsylvania Historical and Museum Commission, 1947). There being no interpretive history of banking in Pennsylvania alone, the reader must extract from Hammond; Fritz Redlich, *The Molding of American Banking: Man and Ideas,* 2 vols. (New York: Hafner, 1951); Ralph and Muriel Hidy, *The House of Baring in American Trade and Finance: English Merchant Bankers at Work 1763–1861* (Cambridge: Harvard University Press, 1949); Nicholas B. Wainwright, *History of the Philadelphia National Bank: A Century and a Half of Philadelphia Banking* (Philadelphia National Bank, 1953); and Vincent Carossa, *Investment Banking in America: A History* (Cambridge: Harvard University Press, 1970). All are scholarly and much concerned with Philadelphia. B. A. Konkle, *Thomas Willing and the First Financial System* (Oxford, England: Oxford University Press, 1937) covers the period of early incorporated banking. There is a long and frustrating two-volume biography, *The Life and Times of Stephen Girard,* by John Bach McMaster (Philadelphia: Lippincott, 1918) and a popular history, *Lonely Midas: the Story of Stephen Girard,* by Harry Emerson Wildes (New York, 1943). For later years there are good biographies by Thomas Payne Govan, *Nicholas Biddle, Nationalist and Public Banker, 1786–1844* (Chicago: University of Chicago Press, 1959) and by Henrietta M. Larson, *Jay Cooke:*

Private Banker (Cambridge: Harvard Studies in Business History, 1936). One of the last national financial leaders from Philadelphia in the nineteenth century, Edwin T. Stotesbury of Drexel, Morgan is treated briefly in James T. Maher, *The Twilight of Splendor: Chronicles of the Age of American Palaces* (Boston: Little, Brown, 1975). Materials for a proper history of the First Bank of the United States are lacking, but that of its successor is well analyzed in Walter B. Smith, *Economic Aspects of the Second Bank of the United States* (Cambridge: Harvard University Press, 1952), as well as in Govan's biography of Biddle. Many aspects of the pioneer development of insurance can be found in highly readable form in Marquis James, *Biography of a Business 1792–1942: Insurance Company of North America* (New York: Bobbs-Merrill, 1942).

The Gilchrist, Pred, and Livingood books have much to say about early east coast transportation. Both transportation and general business development in the western region are included in Catherine Elizabeth Reiser, *Pittsburgh's Commercial Development 1800–1850*. This and George Swetnam's good, brief summary of all forms of transportation in the state were published by the Pennsylvania Historical Association in 1951 and 1964, respectively, and are now available, together with many other studies, from the State Historical and Museum Commission in Harrisburg. The best general survey of the numerous instances of state aid to transportation is Louis Hartz, *Economic Policy and Democratic Thought: Pennsylvania 1776–1860* (Cambridge: Harvard University Press, 1948). There is no scholarly general history of the Pennsylvania Central. The coal roads are discussed in Jules Bogen, *The Anthracite Roads* (New York: New York University Press, 1927) and in William Z. Ripley, *Railroads: Finance and Organization* (London: Longmans, Green, 1915). There are more than half a dozen specialized volumes available from the Historical and Museum Commission on the early logging railroads of the state.

The early interaction of coal, railroads, and iron is well covered in Frederick Moore Binder, *Coal Age Empire: Pennsylvania Coal and its Utilization to 1860* (Harrisburg: Pennsylvania Historical and Museum Commission, 1974), and for the later period in Robert D. Billinger, *Pennsylvania's Coal Industry* (Gettysburg: Pennsylvania Historical Association, 1954).

Since iron was an important product in colonial Pennsylvania, a

reader should start with Arthur Cecil Bining, *Pennsylvania Iron Manufacture in the Eighteenth Century* (Harrisburg: Pennsylvania Historical
and Museum Commission, 2nd ed., 1973). Clark's history of manufactures is slanted toward iron and steel, which means primarily Pennsylvania. James M. Swank, *Progressive Pennsylvania: A Record of
the Remarkable Industrial Development of the Keystone State* (Philadelphia: Lippincott, 1908) is a contemporary account by the secretary
of the national Iron and Steel Institute. For the relations of iron and
steel with other business in the state see Glenn Porter and Harold C.
Livesay, *Merchants and Manufacturers: Studies on the Changing
Structure of Nineteenth Century Marketing* (Baltimore: Johns Hopkins
University Press, 1971). The most recent scholarly view of the industry as a whole is Peter Temin, *Iron and Steel in Nineteenth Century
America: An Economic Inquiry* (Cambridge: M.I.T. Press, 1964). For
other interpretations regarding progress in the industry see W. Paul
Strassman, *Risk and Technological Innovation: American Manufactur-
ing Methods During the Nineteenth Century* (Ithaca, N.Y.: Cornell
University Press, 1959). A detailed analytical biography by Joseph
Frazier Wall, *Andrew Carnegie* (New York: Oxford University Press,
1970), supplies not only the business details of the rise of this colorful
entrepreneur but also a good understanding of the iron and steel industry.

Victor Clark is, of course, useful for the whole range of manufacturing in Pennsylvania, as is Strassman for types of technology. A
boosterish mid-nineteenth-century survey is provided in Edwin T.
Freedley, ed., *Leading Pursuits and Leading Men: A Treatise on the
Principal Trades and Manufactures of the United States* (Philadelphia:
Edward Young, 1856). A similar advertiser-oriented but less useful
book is George H. Thurston, *Pittsburgh's Progress, Industries and
Resources* (Pittsburgh: A. A. Anderson, 1886). Next to coal and iron,
petroleum was, from the early 1860s to the 1890s, the state's most important extractive product. Harold F. Williamson and Arnold Daum,
The American Petroleum Industry: The Age of Illumination 1859–1899
(Evanston, Ill.: Northwestern University Press, 1959) supplies abundant detail on the period, as well as notes and bibliography to facilitate
further reading. Pearce Davis, *The Development of the American
Glass Industry* (Cambridge: Harvard University Press, 1949) is in the
period before 1900 necessarily devoted mainly to Pennsylvania. Ship-

building, always one of the chief activities of the Delaware Valley, is colorfully described in David B. Tyler, *The American Clyde* (Newark, Del.: University of Delaware Press, 1958).

Two of Pennsylvania's major innovative businessmen lack modern scholarly biographies. Andrew Mellon, banker, investor, and developer of aluminum has had only an old eulogy and then a muckraking attack in the 1940s. The account in the *Dictionary of American Biography* is the most reliable source for the essential facts. The same may be said of George Westinghouse, with the qualification that an account of his life collected largely from interviews, Francis E. Leupp, *George Westinghouse* (Boston: Little, Brown, 1918), provides much presumably authentic color and detail that, because of lack of records, can no longer be recovered.

Index

203

974.8
C   Cochran, Thomas C.
       Pennsylvania: A History

	DATE DUE	